Jesus loves the little children

why we baptize children

Daniel R. Hyde

Reformed Fellowship, Inc.
3363 Hickory Ridge Ct. SW
Grandville, MI 49418

Unless otherwise indicated, all Scripture quotations are from
The Holy Bible, English Standard Version, copyright ©2001 by
Crossway Bibles, a division of Good News Publishers. Used by
permission. All rights reserved

Book design by Jeff Steenholdt

For information:
Reformed Fellowship, Inc.
3363 Hickory Ridge Ct. SW
Grandville, MI 49418
Phone: 616.532.8510
Web: reformedfellowship.net
Email: sales@reformedfellowship.net

ISBN 0-9653981-9-6

To Cyprian,
May the waters of baptism ever remind you
to look back upon our Red Sea,
the precious blood of the Son of God,
and forward to the
spiritual land of
Canaan.

Contents

Acknowledgements

Since none of us think and live apart from others, I would like to thank all those who have played a part in this book. To Robert Strimple and Meredith Kline, my most influential professors on the subject of baptism, you took an upstart young Christian and showed him the beauty of Scripture's unity and the significance of my baptism. To the dozens of men, women, and young people whose participation in my membership classes at the Oceanside United Reformed Church has sharpened my ability to present the material in this book. To my elders and deacons for giving me a sabbatical to finish this book. To Debby Rau and Leigh Breckinridge, for their perspectives, both editorial and theological, in making this a readable manuscript. To the Board of the Reformed Fellowship, may your willingness to publish this book result in contributing to a more vibrant faith among our people. And to my helpmeet, Karajean – wife, best friend, conversation partner, and most honest critic – apart from whom my abilities would only be potential.

In nomine Patris, et Filii, et Spiritus Sancti. Amen.
January 2006

Introduction

"Jesus loves the little children,
all the children of the world.
Red and yellow, black and white,
they are precious in his sight.
Jesus loves the little children
of the world."

I can still remember singing those words as a young child growing up in something of a Christian home, albeit a broken home. For anyone who grew up even in the most nominal of Christian homes where these words were present, strong feelings of love for the Lord and confidence in his providential care come to mind when hearing them again.

So what if I said to you that by singing and believing this chorus you believe in infant baptism? Or, if you believe in baby dedication then you believe in infant baptism, but you just don't know it? You'd probably question my sanity. After all, you may reason, the Bible never uses the words "infant baptism" but it does use "dedication." Or you may be thinking, "Infants cannot believe in Jesus so they shouldn't be baptized."

Of all the doctrines and practices of historic Christian churches, whether Eastern Orthodox, Roman Catholic, Lutheran, or Reformed, the baptism of children can be one of the most difficult to wrestle with by those who grew up in non-denominational Protestant churches that did not practice infant baptism. As a Reformed pastor, I've experienced this struggle alongside many of my parishioners and would-be parishioners who either grew up in non-denominational types of churches or were converted in them before they found their way to a Reformed church. Many of them had to endure criticism from family and friends when they became "Calvinists." But at least then their families and friends still considered them Christians. But when these parishioners invited their family and friends to witness the baptism of their children in a worship service, their family and friends began to question their beliefs and wonder if Reformed churches were really just Roman Catholic churches in disguise. Unfortunately this is all too often the case. Misunderstanding and false assumptions abound about infant baptism.

Most today would most likely agree with the great "Prince of Preachers," Charles Haddon Spurgeon, who once said that the practice of infant baptism was nothing more than "Popery."[1] His remark implies that infant baptism is nothing more than a superstitious and man-made doctrine invented by the Roman Catholic Church; as a result, all who perform infant baptism are guilty by association with the Pope – even if they call themselves "Protestants."

What do you think? Is the practice of infant baptism unbiblical? Is it done because of superstition? Was it invented by the Roman Catholic Church? The purpose of this booklet is to give you a clear and concise guide through belief and practice of infant baptism written in a conversational way. The goal in doing so is to demonstrate to you that that it is a biblical practice that is not nor should it be done "out of custom or superstition."[2] As we consider this "hot button" issue, we will look at the Scriptures first and foremost, as they are our ultimate authority. We will also look at some basic biblical and theological principles, the testimony of church history, and finally, some practical matters for the answer to why Reformed churches baptize the children of believers – the children Jesus loves.

---

1. *Metropolitan Tabernacle Pulpit* (Pasadena, Texas: Pilgrim Publications), 19:556.

2. These words come from the address to the parents just before their child is baptized in the traditional Reformed baptismal liturgy of Petrus Dathenus' *Psalter*, first published in 1566. The entire liturgy can be found in "Baptism of Infants: Form Number 1" in either the 1934, 1959, or 1976 editions of the *Psalter Hymnal* (Grand Rapids: Christian Reformed Church) and as "Baptism of Children" in the 1987 edition. See "Appendix 2" for the full text.

Opening Matters

Biblical Presuppositions

Before we tackle the thorny issue of infant baptism, let us first "set the stage," so to speak, by examining some basic Christian and Protestant presuppositions. "Presuppositions" are beliefs we assume before (hence, "pre") we even think about a certain subject. They are the basic "givens" in our mind.

During that great period of church history we call the Protestant Reformation, the Holy Scriptures of the Old and New Testaments were again given the central place in the life of the Church. The Reformers protested against the Church of Rome and its doctrine that the Church's tradition was an equal authority with Scripture by proclaiming the doctrine of *sola scriptura*. *Sola scriptura* means the inspired Scriptures of the Old and New Testaments are the only sufficient and clear rule, guide, and norm of the Church's doctrine and practice, its theology and life.

As the inheritors of this heritage, two of the basic presuppositions all Bible-believing Protestants hold in common, whether they are members of historic Protestant churches or modern-day non-denominational churches, are the doctrines of the *sufficiency* and *perspicuity* of Scripture.

The Sufficiency of Scripture

Many today say things like, "Infant baptism is never taught in the Bible. In fact, the words aren't even in the Bible." While it is true that the term "infant baptism" or an account of a parent bringing their child before a church to be baptized are not *explicitly* found in any specific chapter and verse that says,

"Baptize your children," this does not mean infant baptism is therefore an unbiblical doctrine. Infant baptism is a biblical doctrine because it is a "good and necessary consequence" of the entirety of scriptural teaching. This means that the Scriptures are often like a jigsaw puzzle. One piece by itself does not give a picture of the whole puzzle, yet when many individual pieces are put together a doctrine is necessarily taught.

"But I thought you said the Bible was sufficient?" We have to understand what that term means. When the Protestant Reformers spoke of the Scriptures being "sufficient," they intended this to mean that they taught all that we need to believe and live as Christians in the world, whether a doctrine is taught in an unambiguous, explicit way, *or* by deducing it from several texts and general Christian doctrines. The great Reformed theologian Francis Turretin reflected this understanding of the sufficiency of Scripture when he said, "We acknowledge that many things are to be deduced by legitimate inference and to be considered as the word of God."[3] The fact that something we believe comes from a "good and necessary consequence" does not make it any less true than if it were spelled out explicitly. The best example of this is the doctrine of the Trinity. While there is no verse in Scripture that says, "God is a Trinity and exists as one God in three Persons," we can deduce it from texts that say God is one, as well as that say the Father is God, the Son in God, and the Spirit is God. Another would be the practice of worshipping on Sunday. There is no explicit command in the New Testament to worship on Sunday, yet we do so because this is a good and necessary inference from Scripture (e.g., 1 Cor. 16:2; Rev. 1:10) as well as the practice of the church in the book of Acts.

Historic Protestantism defines this doctrine of the sufficiency

---

3. Francis Turretin, *Institutes of Elenctic Theology*, trans. George Musgrave Giger, ed. James T. Dennison, 3 vols. (Phillipsburg: P&R, 1997), I:135.

of Scripture in no better way than in the words of the Westminster Confession of Faith, written in 1647 by the Reformed ministers and theologians in Great Britain. This Confession of Faith says,

> The whole counsel of God, concerning all things necessary for his own glory, man's salvation, faith, and life, is *either expressly set down in Scripture, or by good and necessary consequence may be deduced from Scripture:* unto which nothing at any time is to be added, whether by new revelations of the Spirit, or traditions of men. (I.6; emphasis added)[4]

In an even more succinct way, article 7 of the Belgic Confession of Faith, written in 1561 by Guy de Brès, says, "We believe that these Holy Scriptures fully contain the will of God, and that whatsoever man ought to believe unto salvation, is sufficiently taught therein."[5]

As God's Word, the Bible is sufficient for our belief and practice about baptism, especially that of infants, because of what it says explicitly and what it says implicitly.

The Perspicuity of Scripture

The second Protestant Reformation presupposition we all hold to is the *perspicuity*, or, the clarity, of Scripture. Again, the Westminster Confession says,

> All things in Scripture are not alike plain in themselves, nor alike clear unto all; yet *those things which are necessary to be known, believed, and observed, for salvation, are so clearly propounded,* and opened in some place of Scripture or other, that not only the learned, but the unlearned, in a due use of the ordinary means, may attain unto a sufficient understanding of them (1:7).[6]

What the perspicuity of Scripture means is that the Scriptures are absolutely clear with regards to salvation: "Believe in the Lord Jesus, and you will be saved" (Acts 16:31).

---

4. *The Creeds of Christendom,* ed. Philip Schaff, rev. David S. Schaff, 3 vols. (reprinted; Grand Rapids: Baker, 1996), III:603. Unless otherwise noted, all references to the Reformed confessions and catechisms are from this volume.

5. *Ibid.,* III:387-8.

6. *Ibid.,* III:604.

Yet not every biblical text or biblical doctrine in the Scriptures are as clear, but take much more study, exegesis, and patience to understand. From the outset of this booklet, we will say that one such doctrine is the doctrine of infant baptism – yet, I hope to show that it is not as "unclear" or mysterious as a doctrine such as the Trinity or a book of the Bible such as Ezekiel or Revelation.

Together, then, we confess the *sufficiency* of Scripture as well as the *perspicuity* of Scripture. You should have noticed that understanding these presuppositions as the Reformers did, and not how they are popularly explained, means that we do not believe a "me and my Bible" type of religion. For while we believe *sola scriptura* – Scripture alone – the Scriptures take great study and patience as well as gifted teachers to explain in many parts. This means that we do not approach God's Word as if we were the first people to read and interpret it. In fact, we draw upon 2000 years of study, exegesis, reflection, and interpretation that testify to the truths of Scripture. And so the history of the Church is a valuable tool for us to look to in confirming biblical study as well as keeping our interpretation of Scripture from deviating from the historic consensus of churches, learned pastors, teachers, and theologians.

Christian Charity

One final matter that we must presuppose is that of communication. We must communicate to each other well and not talk past one another. This is not only necessary as men and women, but as *Christians*. As we discuss infant baptism, we are mindful that it is our responsibility as Christians to be "eager to maintain the unity of the Spirit in the bond of peace" (Eph. 4:3). This peace that we have been given by God we are to pass to each other. Notice how Paul goes on to explain what this unity and peace looks like when he says,

> There is one body and one Spirit - just as you were called to the one hope that belongs to your call - one Lord, one faith, *one*

baptism, one God and Father of all, who is over all and through all and in all." (Eph. 4:4-6)

It is this "one baptism" that unites the members of Christ's Church and that we are to be "eager" to understand and apply to our lives.

So how do we do strive for unity as Christians on this vital subject? Paul goes on in another place about the Church having one mouth, with one voice. In Romans 15:5-6 he prays for the Christians in Rome, saying,

> May the God of endurance and encouragement grant you to live in such *harmony* with one another, in accord with Christ Jesus, that together you may with *one voice* glorify the God and Father of our Lord Jesus Christ.

In these words Paul bases our like-mindedness, our "harmony," with each other upon God's attribute of long-suffering. *He* is patient; therefore *we* ought to be patient with each other.

Paul elsewhere passionately pleads for this like-mindedness among Christians, saying,

> So if there is any encouragement in Christ, any comfort from love, any participation in the Spirit, any affection and sympathy, complete my joy by being *of the same mind*, having the *same love*, being in *full accord* and of *one mind*. Do nothing from rivalry or conceit, but in humility count others more significant than yourselves. Let each of you look not only to his own interests, but also to the interests of others (Phil. 2:1-4).

As those who have been encouraged in Christ, comforted by his love for us and the love of the family of God for us, and united together by the same Spirit, we are to defer to others as we fulfill the apostle's joy by being like-minded.

In this book we are seeking to do precisely what the Word of God calls us to do – be united. Here we are not trying to find out who is right and who is wrong simply to win a debate or an argument, but we are by the power of the Spirit seeking to become one in Christ and to express that visibly in the biblical act of unity, baptism.

Defining Our Terms

As Christians who are seeking the truth of God's Word together in genuine charity as a means to become one in heart, will, and voice, let us begin to do that by coming to a consensus on certain words and phrases that will be used in this book. This is imperative if we are to avoid the potential misunderstandings inherent in a discussion of infant baptism. And so for us to be able to discuss infant baptism and all that it entails, we must first speak the same language.

Baptism

The first and most obvious term we need to define and understand together is the subject of this book, "baptism." Historically speaking, Christians and the Protestant Reformers understood baptism as the visible initiation into the Church of Jesus Christ by means of the outward sign of water.

Jesus instituted baptism after his resurrection and just before his ascension into heaven in Matthew 28. Along with teaching the nations, baptism was to be a perpetual ordinance, as Jesus promised to be with his Church "to the end of the age" (Matt. 28:20). It was given for the benefit of his New Covenant people, just as circumcision had been given to the people of God in the Old Testament (Gen. 17). Like circumcision, baptism is the visible sign of initiation into a covenant relationship with the Lord. Notice how this is shown in Matthew 28:19 as "making disciples" is defined with two verbs, "baptizing" and "teaching." One is made a disciple, that is, a follower of Christ, by baptism and instruction.[7] Paul says that by baptism we are incorporated in the body of

Christ, the Church, when he says,

> For just as the body is one and has many members, and all the members of the body, though many, are one body, so it is with Christ. For in one Spirit we were all baptized into one body—Jews or Greeks, slaves or free—and all were made to drink of one Spirit (1 Cor. 12:12-13).

Baptism, then, has been understood as the rite (outward ceremonial action[8]) of passage distinguishing the children of God from the unbelieving world by graciously incorporating them into Christ's covenant community. This is why article 34 of the aforementioned Belgic Confession of Faith, says that by baptism "we are received into the Church of God, and separated from all other people and strange religions, that we may wholly belong to him whose ensign and banner we bear."[9]

Baptism by water, then, is the means by which God "put[s] a visible difference between those that belong unto the Church and the rest of the world" (Westminster Confession of Faith, 27.1).

Sacraments

Baptism, along with the Lord's Supper, has also been called by the historic Christian Church a "sacrament." Before thinking that this is a Roman Catholic idea, listen to how the great

---

7. This point was highlighted by the Reformer of Zurich, Switzerland, Ulrich Zwingli, in 1525 in his treatise, *Of Baptism. Zwingli and Bullinger*, ed. G.W. Bromiley, *Library of Christian Classics* (Philadelphia: Westminster, 1953), 143-4.

8. The Second Helvetic Confession, written in 1566 by Heinrich Bullinger, calls the sacraments "mystical symbols, or holy rites, or sacred actions" (ch. 19.1). *The Creeds of Christendom*, III:884. Peter J. Leithart speaks of baptism as "a rite of entry that expresses the character of the church – that it is a community where racial, economic, and sexual divisions are dissolved (1 Cor. 12:12-13, Gal. 3:27-29)." *Calvin Theological Journal* 40:1 (April 2005): 18.

9. *The Creeds of Christendom*, III:425; cf. Second Helvetic Confession, ch. 19.1, which says the sacraments were ordained by God "whereby he does separate us from all other people and religions." *The Creeds of Christendom*, III:884.

Heidelberg Catechism[10] explains what a sacrament is. This Catechism was published in 1563 in the Protestant region of Germany known as the Palatinate in order to explain the Christian Faith in a time of political and theological chaos. It answers the question of what the sacraments are, saying,

> The Sacraments are visible, holy signs and seals, appointed of God for this end, that by the use thereof he may the more fully declare and seal to us the promise of the Gospel; namely, that he grants us out of free grace the forgiveness of sins and everlasting life, for the sake of the one sacrifice of Christ accomplished on the cross (Q&A 66).[11]

The original use of the Latin term *sacramentum* was as an oath of allegiance by Roman soldiers. Yet what is so amazing about the above answer is that it explains the oath as *God's* oath to us: "*he* may the more fully declare and seal to us the promise of the Gospel." The two sacraments of baptism and the Lord's Supper,[12] then, are the visible *signs* in which God shows us his grace in a tangible way. They are also *seals*, that is, the official stamp of God's promise that he is our God and we are his people. This language of "sign" and "seal" as God's oath to us comes directly from Paul's description of circumcision in Romans 4:10, where he speaks of the "sign of circumcision" being "a seal of the righteousness that he had by faith." God gave the outward picture as a confirmation of what Abraham had by faith – the righteousness of Jesus Christ.

Another way to think of the sacraments is that they are visible signs of an invisible reality. The Belgic Confession, article 33, defines a sacrament by saying, "For they are visible

---

10. "Catechism" is the English word for the Greek word *katecheo*, which simply means "oral teaching/instruction." From the ancient Church until now, God's people have been instructed in the faith by way of question and answer (Ex. 12:26-27, 13:14-16; Josh. 4:21-24; Luke 1:4).

11. *The Creeds of Christendom*, III:328; cf. Westminster Confession of Faith, 27.1

12. Heidelberg Catechism, Q&A 68; Belgic Confession of Faith, art. 33; Westminster Confession of Faith, 27.4

signs and seals of an inward and invisible thing."[13] Sacraments have a "sign" and a "thing signified."[14] In defining sacraments in this way, the Reformation tradition was following the definition of St. Augustine (A.D. 354-430), who called the sacraments "visible words."[15]

To illustrate this, think about love. Can you touch, taste, or see it? No, but a groom gives his wife a wedding ring as a visible sign that he loves her and is committed to her. This symbolism applies to the doctrine of baptism. The children of believing parents are a part of God's covenant family. This is the invisible reality, or truth. The outward sign of baptism visibly shows that this invisible reality is true.

Although when many of us hear the word "sacrament," we immediately think of Roman Catholicism, it is not "Catholic" to believe there are sacraments. Roman Catholicism teaches that baptism washes away all sins, original and actual, while giving the sanctifying grace of justification which enables the baptized to believe and live a life in the Spirit.[16] This is accomplished *ex opere operato*; that is, by simply performing the act the work of washing away sin is done. As Protestants we reject this teaching because we believe we are justified through faith alone, by God's grace alone, because of Christ's work alone. Infant baptism, like adult baptism, does not wash away sins or justify a person. The Heidelberg Catechism speaks to this when it says,

> Is, then, the outward washing of water itself the washing away of sins?
>
> No; for only the blood of Jesus Christ and the Holy Spirit cleanse us from all sin (Q&A 72).[17]

As a sacrament, baptism visually signifies and seals the promise of the Gospel – which must be received by faith.

---

13. *The Creeds of Christendom*, III:424.
14. Westminster Confession of Faith, 27:1. *Ibid.*, III:660-1.
15. *Reply to Faustus the Manichaean*, ch. 19; *Tractates on John*, LXXX.3.
16. Catechism of the Catholic Church (New York: Doubleday, 1994), 353-4.
17. *The Creeds of Christendom*, III:330; cf. Westminster Confession of Faith, 27.4.

Therefore we speak of the preaching of the Gospel and sacraments as the "means of grace." It is by these means that the Holy Spirit communicates to us the grace of God for the creation (preaching of the Gospel) and confirmation (sacraments) of our faith.[18]

Grace

If baptism is a sacrament that visibly portrays and promises grace, what, then, is grace? The grace of God is his favorable attitude towards sinners despite their having done nothing to earn it (unmerited favor) and despite their having done everything to forfeit it (de-merited favor). This is why Paul says, "For by grace you have been saved" (Eph. 2:8). We have done nothing to earn it, for it is "not a result of works, so that no one may boast" (Eph. 2:8), and in fact, we have done everything to forfeit it, as we followed "the course of this world," we followed "the prince of the power of the air," and we lived "in the passions of our flesh, carrying out the desires of the body and the mind" (Eph. 2:2-3).

Grace, then, we can say, is like the love we show to our children. We love them from the time we find out they have been conceived, even though at that point in time they have done nothing to deserve or earn our love. As they grow, they may openly disobey us and forfeit all right to be loved, yet we still love them regardless.

Covenant

This grace of God does not come to us out of the clear blue sky, though. It comes to us within a certain context. This context is what we call a covenant relationship. As Paul says, the Gentiles were at one time "strangers to the covenants of promise" (Eph. 2:12). To be in such a state meant to be unloved and outside the grace of God. Let us consider what the word "covenant" means.

---

18. See Heidelberg Catechism, Q&A 65.

A covenant is a solemn bond initiated by one party with another party. To illustrate this, think of how the President covenants, or solemnly agrees, to increase federal funding for public schools. He makes this agreement (covenant) and then to show his solemn agreement to do so he signs the bill into law and confirms it by placing the official seal of the office of the President (sacrament). This official seal (sacrament) signifies to all that read this bill that the President has agreed (covenanted) to do this. God promises to save all that believe in Jesus Christ; this is his covenant. He confirms this with his official seals – his sacraments.

A covenant is a bond or a promise. God made his covenant with Abraham by promising that his descendants would be as the sand of the sea and the stars of the sky (Gen. 15:5). The covenant sign of circumcision (sacrament), then, showed him that the LORD's word was as good as gold.

The Covenant of Grace

Believers through all ages have received this grace, and are thereby members of the "covenant of grace." Remember that we said a covenant is a solemn bond initiated by one party with another party and that grace is God's attitude towards sinners despite their having done nothing to earn it (unmerited favor) and despite having done everything to forfeit it (de-merited favor). The "covenant of grace," then, is the grace of God, which he began unfolding to his people in the Garden, and will continue to unfold until the dawn of the New Heavens and New Earth. God's one plan of salvation, his "covenant," is progressively revealed and unfolded through many individual covenant arrangements. All these we call the one "covenant of grace."

This covenant of grace began in the Garden and will continue until our Lord returns. Our gracious God first made this covenant of grace with our fallen parents in the Garden when he spoke of the promise of a "seed." He told Adam and Eve, "I will put enmity between you (the serpent) and the woman, and between your offspring and her offspring; he shall bruise your head, and you shall bruise his heel" (Gen. 3:15). He later elaborated upon it in the form of covenants with Noah, then with the patriarchs Abraham, Isaac, and Jacob, then with Moses, and to all his people until the Lord Jesus Christ came. In a sense we can speak of the covenants, or the one all-encompassing covenant of grace, as the process by which the LORD watered this "seed" promise until it became a full-grown tree in the New Covenant brought by Jesus Christ.

Our Heidelberg Catechism, in Q&A 19, summarizes this great history of God's covenant of grace by saying that it was

> ...first revealed in Paradise, afterwards proclaimed by the holy Patriarchs and Prophets, and foreshadowed by the sacrifices and other ceremonies of the law, and finally fulfilled by his well-beloved Son.[19]

The Westminster Confession of Faith summarizes this history of salvation in these words:

> Although the work of redemption was not actually wrought by Christ till after his incarnation, yet the virtue, efficacy, and benefits thereof were communicated into the elect, in all ages successively from the beginning of the world, in and by those promises, types, and sacrifices, wherein he was revealed, and signified to be the seed of the woman, which should bruise the serpent's head, and the lamb slain from the beginning of the world, being yesterday and today the same and forever (VIII.6).[20]

In summary, then, when we approach the biblical topic of baptism, we must have a common vocabulary. We speak with one voice when we understand and say that baptism is the sacramental sign and seal of God's wonderful, covenantal grace in which our loving Father has revealed his Son to his people.

---

19. *The Creeds of Christendom*, III:313.
20. *Ibid.*, III:621-2.

Circumcision & Baptism

Hopefully now we are on the same page. We believe the Bible is God's Word, and it speaks to us authoritatively about what we are to believe in order to be saved and how we are to live in light of that knowledge as Christians. We desire to communicate in a godly way that seeks and promotes the unity of the body of Christ. And now we have an appreciation for terms like "sacrament" and "covenant of grace." Now *all* that remains is to agree on the answer to the question, "Why do Reformed churches baptize the children of professing believers?"

The Meaning of Old Testament Circumcision

As we've already said in passing, the New Covenant sign of initiation into the covenant people of God, baptism, has an Old Testament counterpart, circumcision. This is mentioned because for us to understand the meaning of baptism it is crucial to know the meaning of circumcision.

Circumcision was both an oath-curse, "I will be your God," as well as the sign of consecration to the Lord of the covenant of grace, "You will be my people."

Sign of Curse

Circumcision was an outward oath in which a curse was involved. It was a symbolic judgment through which all male members of the covenant had to pass. While God swore the oath, "I will be your God," this oath was ratified, put into effect, by cutting off the foreskin of the male reproductive organ. This symbolized that if either God or the people broke the covenant, they would be cut off from the people and under a curse (Gen. 17:14). And in the case of the people, their offspring would be cut off as well, as the significance of the reproductive organ signifies. This is why earlier, in Genesis 15, Abraham saw the strange vision of the Lord of the covenant passing through the hewn animal carcasses. God was himself making the oath that if he failed to lead his people into what he had promised, he would be cut off. And so the seriousness of not receiving the sign of the covenant, which meant one was a covenant breaker (Gen. 17:14), was re-iterated throughout redemptive history (Ex. 4:24-26; Josh. 5:2ff).

Sign of Consecration

Circumcision also included the aspect of the blessing of God as it signified the people's consecration to their covenant king. When Isaac, the son of promise, was born, Abraham circumcised him on the eighth day as God commanded (Gen. 21:4). But later Abraham was summoned to cut Isaac off altogether (Gen. 22). God said Isaac was to be offered as a "burnt offering" (Gen. 22:2), the type of sacrifice that expressed a total consecration. Thus Abraham was confronted with the dilemma of circumcision as consecration, for he who would be consecrated to God can do so only by passing through the judgment that circumcision symbolizes.[21]

Covenant Sign

Circumcision was given to Abraham in the context of a covenant. In the ancient Near East, covenants were ratified when the king and his subjects made sacred oaths, and dramatically symbolized them in solemn rites using a knife (Gen. 15, 17).[22] Circumcision, then, followed the general pattern of covenants in the ancient Near East. The basic pattern was as follows: **historical preamble**, in which the king (the

---

21. Meredith G. Kline, *By Oath Consigned* (reprinted; Eugene: Wipf & Stock, 1998), 44-5.
22. Meredith G. Kline, "Genesis," *The New Bible Commentary* (Grand Rapids: Eerdmans, 1970), 96.

suzerain) would chronicle who he was and what he had done for his subjects (the vassals). We see this in the following words: "I am the LORD who brought you out from Ur of the Chaldeans...I am God Almighty" (Gen. 15:7; 17:1). Then the king would give the **stipulations** of the covenant relationship, in which he would promise to do certain things, while his subjects were told what their obligations were. With circumcision God promised "to be God to you and your offspring after you" (Gen. 17:7), while his people were obligated to "walk before me and be blameless" (Gen. 17:1). Finally the king would list the **sanctions** of the covenant: if his subjects were obedient he would bless them, but if they were disobedient he would curse them. This is seen in the curse/consecration aspect of circumcision mentioned above.

So circumcision was the outward "sign of the covenant" (Gen. 17:11) that existed between the LORD and his people. This is so important for us to realize because circumcision was not merely a sign of Israel's temporal and/or national blessings. This is often a misperception. Circumcision also was not just some outward way to distinguish Israel ethnically from the other nationalities around them. What this means is that when a Jewish boy was circumcised on the eighth day, or a convert to Israel's faith in the LORD was circumcised, this was not the end of the significance of circumcision.

Circumcision was deeply religious and spiritual and not just a physical act. The blessing/consecration aspect of circumcision is highlighted throughout Scripture. For example, in Romans 2:28-29 Paul says circumcision is not "outward and physical," but instead it is a "matter of the heart, by the Spirit, not by the letter." Thus it is the outward sign of the most significant spiritual blessings that those who trusted in the Lord Jesus Christ alone by faith alone received. This is why in the text we've already mentioned, Romans 4:11, Paul says that Abraham "received the sign of circumcision as a seal of the righteousness that he had by faith." Circumcision was to the Jews the outward sign of the blessings our gracious God gives to unworthy sinners: regeneration (Rom. 2:29) and justification (Rom. 4:11).[23]

Going back into the pages of the Old Testament this truth of circumcision having a deeply spiritual meaning is clearly found. The prophet Jeremiah chastised the LORD's son, Israel (Ex. 4:22), pointing out that receiving the *external sign* of circumcision was not the purpose of circumcision. Because of their attitude and unbelief they had become *spiritually* uncircumcised and therefore grouped together with the unclean Gentiles – despite their outward circumcision:

> Behold, the days are coming, declares the LORD, when I will punish all those who are circumcised merely in the flesh – Egypt, Judah, Edom, the sons of Ammon, Moab, and all who dwell in the desert who cut the corners of their hair, for all these nations are uncircumcised, and all the house of Israel is uncircumcised in heart (Jer. 9:25-26).

Listen to how the following Scripture texts from the Old Testament describe circumcision. First, it was a sign of the heart that confessed its sin and iniquity (Lev. 26:40-42); second, it was a sign of a circumcised/sanctified heart (Deut. 10:16); and third, it was a sign of the work of God's grace in the heart of those sinners whom the LORD would re-gather from exile because of their disobedience (Deut. 30:6). Notice how this promise of being re-gathered into the land of promise was explained later by Ezekiel as coinciding with a spiritual re-birth:

> I will take you from the nations and gather you from all the countries and bring you into your own land. I will sprinkle clean water on you, and you shall be clean from all your uncleannesses, and from all your idols I will cleanse you. And I will give you a new heart, and a new spirit I will put within you. And I will remove the heart of stone from your flesh and give you a heart of flesh. And I will put my Spirit within you, and cause you to walk in my statutes and be careful to obey my rules (Ezek. 36:24-27).

Finally, the Old Testament even describes circumcision as a

---

23. See St. Augustine, *City of God*, 16:27.

sign of what Paul would later describe in the New Testament as the putting off the old man, and the putting on the new man (Jer. 4:4, 9:26; Ezek. 44:7 cf. Eph. 4:22-24; Col. 3:5-14).

"Christian Circumcision"

Why is it important to understand that circumcision meant more than just the physical act, but had a deeply spiritual purpose? Because by doing so we can see that the meaning of circumcision was essentially the same as that of baptism.[24] And so as Reformed churches we teach that circumcision and baptism are equated in the Scriptures.

The Old Testament sign and rite of initiation into the covenant community, circumcision, signified the same spiritual blessings as the New Covenant sign and rite of baptism. The great difference is that in the New Covenant the outward sign has been changed from a bloody sacrament to an unbloody sacrament. Christ is our bloody circumcision on the cross, having been cut in two, so to speak, on the cross as the animals in ancient covenant ceremonies (Isa. 52:13-53:12; Dan. 9:25-27; Col. 2:11). As a result there is no longer any significance to circumcision for the Christian (Gal. 5:1-15).[25]

Like circumcision, baptism is explained in the New Testament as the sign of the highest spiritual blessings that God gives to sinners. First, baptism is generally spoken of as the sign of the saving work of God (Acts 16:30ff); second, specifically, baptism is spoken of as the sign of the forgiveness of sins

---

24. This is taught in the Westminster Confession of Faith 27:5, which says, "The sacraments of the Old Testament, in regard of the spiritual things thereby signified and exhibited, were, for substance, the same with those of the New." *The Creeds of Christendom*, III:661.

25. See the Belgic Confession, article 34, which says, "We believe and confess that Jesus Christ, who is the end of the law, hath made an end, by the shedding of his blood, of all other sheddings of blood which men could or would make as a propitiation or satisfaction for sin; and that he, having abolished circumcision, which was done with blood, hath instituted the Sacrament of Baptism instead thereof." *The Creeds of Christendom*, III:425.

(Acts 2:38); third, of the washing away of our innumerable sins (Acts 22:16); fourth, of the renewal that we have in Christ (Rom. 6:4); fifth, of our having put on Christ (Gal. 3:28); sixth, of the washing of regeneration and renewal (Titus 3:5,[26]; Eph. 5:23) by the power of the Holy Spirit (Acts 1:5); seventh, of being united to the community of faith by the Spirit (1 Cor. 12:13); and, eighth, of being united to Christ, clothed with Christ, right with God by faith, Abraham's seed, and heirs of God's promises (Gal. 3:26-29).

So just like circumcision, baptism was never intended to be an outward sign only, but was to point us to even greater realities: that God gives new life; that God justifies; that God saves! These ceremonial signs do not save in and of themselves but teach us to cling to the grace of God as found in Jesus Christ.

Thus we come to Colossians 2:11-12 in which Paul not only equates circumcision and baptism, but shows that baptism has replaced circumcision in the New Covenant era,[27] when he says,

> In him also you were circumcised with a circumcision made without hands, by putting off the body of the flesh, by the circumcision of Christ, having been buried with him in baptism, in which you were also raised with him through faith in the powerful working of God, who raised him from the dead (Col. 2:11-12).

Paul is teaching that the Christian is already "full" and complete in Christ, and does not need anything to make him or her more spiritual (Col. 2:9-10). He says that we *have* been circumcised, but not with human hands. Here he is speaking of

---

26. Here Paul links the sign (washing, i.e., baptism) with the thing signified (regeneration, renewal) and makes it clear that the effectual agent who accomplishes both regeneration and renewal is the Holy Spirit, who is poured out through Jesus Christ. Cf. *John Calvin Commentaries on the Epistle to Titus*, trans. William Pringle, *Calvin's Commentaries*, 22 vols. (Grand Rapids: Baker, reprinted 1996), XXI:382-3.

27. See also the Heidelberg Catechism, Q&A 74 and Belgic Confession, article 34.

the spiritual reality we have received, of which we saw the Old Testament speak concerning circumcision. The spiritual reality was a "putting off the body of the flesh," which means new birth. The body of the flesh is the sinful nature that enslaved us and consumed us. To put it off means it no longer dominates us. It has been killed and we have been made alive. All this Paul calls "the circumcision of Christ."

The question is what is the "circumcision" to which he refers? There are two ways to interpret the grammar of the phrase "circumcision of Christ." It can be understood as Christ's circumcision, that is, his crucifixion as he was "cut off" in the knife ritual we mentioned with Genesis 15 and 17 above. The other way of understanding this phrase is that it is a circumcision "done by Christ" (NIV) upon us as his people. It is the Christian's circumcision, that is, his being identified with Christ in his cross. What is important to note is that this understanding does not exclude the first interpretation because our circumcision in baptism is an identification with Christ's being circumcised on the cross as he bore the curse of our covenant breaking and was thus "cut off" in order that our transgressions of the covenant might be forgiven and cancelled (Col. 2:13-14) and that we might be liberated from the power of the devil and his armies (Col. 2:15).

So when were we circumcised by Christ? In verse 12 the apostle gives the explanation, basically saying, "You were circumcised when you were baptized."[28] This is why we no longer need to undergo the ritual of circumcision to make us full members of Christ or his Church. And so the sign of the New Testament is said here to replace the sign of the Old, circumcision. This is why Paul could say in Philippians 3:3,

---

28. Justin Martyr made this point in his *Dialog with Trypho the Jew*, ch. 18, saying, "Wash therefore, and be now clean, and put away iniquity from your souls, as God bids you be washed in this laver, and be circumcised with the true circumcision."

dramatically, "For we are the real circumcision, who worship by the Spirit of God." What Paul is saying is that the New Testament Church as a whole is characterized as those who have been circumcised truly. And according to his words in Colossians 2:11-12, to be circumcised is to be baptized.

Baptism as Sign of Curse and Consecration

As we think of baptism along the lines of circumcision, we are struck by the fact that baptism is also sign of curse/consecration. For those who believe in what baptism signifies, it is a sign and seal of their blessing in Christ, but for those who reject what baptism signifies, it is a sign and seal of their judgment as covenant breakers.

So we can speak of both circumcision and baptism as the visible signs and seals of their respective covenant people. And we have seen that they signify, or represent, the same things. Furthermore, because baptism replaces circumcision the children of believers are to be baptized in the New Covenant just as they were to be circumcised in the Old Testament.

We get a glimpse of how Paul saw circumcision and baptism as essentially the same in his statement in 1 Corinthians 10:2. In speaking of our "forefathers" he says "...all were baptized into Moses in the cloud and in the sea." We might say that this is *the* proof-text that teaches infant baptism! They who were circumcised and went through the Sea (Ex. 12:37) were "baptized" just as we who have been baptized have been circumcised. The context of this statement is Paul's parallel between Israel, in their days of Exodus, salvation, and wilderness life, and the New Covenant people of God, who are to view their forefathers in the faith as "examples" (Greek, *tupoi*, "types"). What Paul is saying is that there is an analogous relationship between Israel's experience and the Church's, so much so that the apostle can speak of the generation under the leadership of Moses as participating in signs and seals that corresponded to the Church's sacraments of baptism and the Lord's Supper.[29] And so the Church is the continuation of Israel as the covenant people of God. And as the covenant people of God, they receive the sign of the covenant. Like circumcision, Israel's passing through the Red Sea was an "ordeal" of cursing and blessing: Egypt was cursed while Israel was blessed.[30] This is how Paul speaks of this passing through the Red Sea as a "baptism," even though it occurred in the Old Testament. As well, it was a baptism because like the Church, Israel's "baptism" had a corporate aspect to it. Baptism "into Moses" means sharing the destiny of the covenant mediator, Moses, by participating in his deliverance from Egypt through the waters of the Red Sea, while baptism into Christ (cf. Rom. 6:3), our covenant mediator who went through the curse on behalf of his people, means sharing his destiny of deliverance from the curse of death and being cut-off from God in his glorious resurrection.[31]

As well, Peter understood baptism to be a sign of curse and consecration by comparing it to the Flood (1 Peter 3:20-22).[32] In this passage, Christian baptism is directly designated as the "antitype" (Greek, *antitupon*; v. 21) of the ordeal waters of the Flood.

It is important to note that the NIV's rendering of *antitype* as "this water *symbolizes* baptism that now saves you" is not as accurate as the NASB or the ESV, which say, "And corresponding to that, baptism now saves you," and "Baptism,

---

29. Kline, *By Oath Consigned*, 67-8.
30. This point was mentioned by the ancient church fathers Tertullian, in *On Baptism*, ch. 9, and Ambrose, *in On the Mysteries*, ch. 3.12.
31. C. K. Barrett, *The First Epistle to the Corinthians* (San Francisco: Harper, 1968), 221.
32. See Tertullian, *On Baptism*, ch. 8. Also interesting is how the blessing aspect of water is brought out by Tertullian (*On Baptism*, ch. 3) and Ambrose (*On the Mysteries*, ch. 3.9) by seeing a type of baptism in the waters of the original creation, which brought forth life.

which corresponds to this," respectively. Peter's point is that the waters of the Flood foreshadowed the waters of baptism. As Noah was delivered from judgment by the waters of the flood, so too, we are delivered from God's judgment by the waters of baptism, though, as Peter notes in the next clause, it is not the mere sign (the washing with water) that saves, but baptism saves because it is connected to the resurrection of Christ (v. 21), and a clean conscience before God (v. 21), that is, the reality that is signified by the ordeal-sign of the washing with water. The sign and the thing *signified* are both in view here. As Calvin said on this verse,

> The meaning, however, is not ambiguous, that Noah, saved by water, had a sort of baptism. And this the apostle mentions, that the likeness between him and us might appear more evident...As Noah, then, obtained life through death, when in the ark, he was enclosed not otherwise than as it were in the grave, and when the whole world perished, he was preserved together with his small family; so at this day, the death which is set forth in baptism, is to us an entrance into life, nor can salvation be hoped for, except we be separated from the world...We ought to acknowledge in baptism a spiritual washing, we ought to embrace therein the testimony of the remission of sin and the pledge of our renovation, and yet so as to leave to Christ his own honour, and also to the Holy Spirit; so that no part of our salvation should be transferred to the sign.[33]

Thus it is important to note that a water-ordeal indicates blessing or curse for the one going through the waters. Blessing comes for those who are justified by grace alone by embracing the promise of baptism through faith alone. Christians enter the waters of destruction believing that God will deliver them and their children by bringing them safely through very element which he will use to bring judgment upon unbelievers.

---

33. John Calvin *Commentaries on the Epistle of Paul the Apostle to the Hebrews*, trans. John Owen, *Calvin's Commentaries*, 22 vols. (Grand Rapids: Baker, reprinted 1996), XXII:116, 117, 118.

This is why Peter can appeal to Noah and his family, who were "saved through the waters." Curse, on the other hand, comes to those who enter the waters without faith and who are swallowed up and consumed by the waters of judgment, the home of leviathan and the dragon.

The Example of Abraham

At this point we need to pause and reflect on what this means. When we see that circumcision and baptism are the signs of the Old and New Testaments, that they taught essentially the same things, and that baptism replaces circumcision, we have to say that every argument a person can give against infant baptism in the New Testament can also be said of infant circumcision in the Old Testament.[34]

While we have said that baptism is a sign of God's saving grace, *baptism does not necessarily follow chronologically after a sinner is saved*, as the Westminster Confession of Faith states in chapter 28:6, "The efficacy of baptism is not tied to the moment of time wherein it is administered."[35] Since baptism is a tangible way that we have experienced the grace and mercy of God in Christ, it can be a very emotional aspect of our experience as Christians. Many of those for whom this booklet is intended were baptized as adults in a public setting. I share the same experience. Yet we must not think that our personal experience of testifying to God's grace before many fellow believers is the litmus test of anyone's theology of baptism. While baptism can be an intensely moving experience, it doesn't mean that adult baptism is the best way or the only way God intends this sacrament to be used. The sacrament of

---

34. This was also stated by John Calvin, *Institutes of the Christian Religion*, ed. John T. McNeill, trans. Ford Lewis Battles, *Library of Christian Classics*, 2 vols. (Philadelphia: The Westminster Press, 1960), 4:16:9, 29.

35. *The Creeds of Christendom*, III:663; Cornelis P. Venema, "Sacraments and Baptism in the Reformed Confessions." *Mid-America Journal of Theology* 11 (2000): 82.

baptism and God's grace are no less meaningful or powerful when placed upon a child in the presence of his parents, grandparents, and fellow brothers and sisters in Christ or in the life of a child who grows up in a Christian home and never knowing a day when they consciously did not experience the presence and grace of the Lord Jesus Christ. Just think of Timothy, of whom Paul says in 2 Timothy 3:15, "from childhood you have been acquainted with the sacred writings, which are able to make you wise for salvation through faith in Jesus Christ."

That being said, again, the New Testament does not teach that there is necessarily a chronologically simultaneous relationship between the reception of the sacraments and its spiritual benefits. Consider the way a person hears the Word preached. That person may hear hundreds of sermons before ever receiving the benefits promised in the preached Word. I, for one, can testify to this. I grew up in a Christian home, heard Bible stories, attended Sunday school, prayed with my family, heard the Scriptures read, but did not consciously come to faith until I was over 17 years old. Are we then to conclude that everyone must undergo years of hearing the Word first and before coming to faith? The answer is no. One's personal experience is not to become the doctrine of the Church. But this is what has happened with baptism. My conversion and baptism were very emotional experiences. But just because it happened to me in this way doesn't mean it must for another. Just as the Word of the gospel might be preached to someone at one point but the benefit of salvation may come at a much later point, so too it is with baptism. A long period of time may pass between the time a child receives baptism and the time God brings that child to a saving knowledge of the truth of which baptism is a picture.

When we say that baptism is a sign of already-being-saved we forget that what is so amazing about the story of Abraham. In Romans 4:11 we are told that Abraham's circumcision was a seal of the righteousness that comes by faith. Abraham was a believer already. As Genesis 15:6 says, "He believed the LORD, and he counted it to him as righteousness." So he was circumcised *after* he believed. But what did God then command Abraham to do in Genesis 17? He was commanded to administer the sign of circumcision to his seed.[36] As the story unfolds, Abraham takes his son Ishmael, all those born in his household and household servants, and circumcises them. Later, after Isaac is born, Abraham circumcises him although he is only eight days old and has given absolutely no indication that he believed already. Abraham, then, was circumcising people *before* they professed faith in the LORD. Circumcision was still a sign of the righteousness that comes by faith, but since there is not a simultaneous relationship, the sign could be given first, then latter in Isaac's life the blessing of the sign, righteousness by faith, could come. We, as Abraham's children (Gal. 3:7), need to follow Abraham's example. Although we may not understand how a baby can be baptized now and come to faith later, this is how God has worked throughout history. He did it then and he can do it now – he does do it now!

Thus God's covenant sign of baptism is to be given to the children of believers because it has replaced circumcision. The same "seed" or descendants of Abraham that were circumcised in the Old Testament are the same "seed" that are now baptized. As we have seen above in the equating of circumcision and baptism: "The *essence* of the sign was never abolished. The *form* was."[37] This means that God's grace is the same throughout the covenants, although the sign is different: circumcision then, baptism now.

---

36. This point was already made by St. Augustine in *On Baptism, Against the Donatists*, IV:461-2.

37. Herman Hoeksema, T*he Biblical Ground for the Baptism of Infants* (First Protestant Reformed Church: Grand Rapids, reprinted 1990), 21. Cf. B.B. Warfield, "*Christian Baptism." Selected Shorter Writings of Benjamin B. Warfield,* ed. John E. Meeter, 2 vols. (Phillipsburg: P&R, 1970), I:326-7

Covenant & Baptism

To recap, the God who reveals himself in the Bible is a covenant making God and has and brought his people into a relationship with himself by making covenants with them. He has been a covenant making God in the past and he always will be a covenant making God. And when he makes a covenant between himself and his people he always gives a sign of that covenant. For example, in the Garden of Eden he gave the tree of life (Gen. 2:9); to Noah and the rest of the earth he gave the rainbow (Gen. 9:13); to Abraham he gave circumcision (Gen. 17:10); to Israel he gave the Sabbath (Ex. 31:13) and the Passover (Ex. 12), among others; and to the Church he gave baptism (Matt. 28:19) and Lord's Supper (Matt. 26:26-29). These sacraments were meant to signify visibly and to seal inwardly, that is, to confirm, the blessings of having a relationship with God.

All too often in discussions about baptism and infant baptism, we lose focus of the big picture of Scripture. Simply "proof-texting" back and forth will not do. With that said, we move into a discussion here of the "big picture" of Scripture. Baptism does not occur in isolation from what goes on in the unfolding drama of God's redemptive plan, but it is intimately linked with the overall context of God's covenant relationship with his people. Apart from this overall context of the Old and New Testaments, it is nearly impossible even to speak clearly to each other about baptism.

The Unity of the People of God in the Old and New Testaments

The big picture of circumcision and baptism is the unity of God's covenant relationships throughout the Old and New Testaments. There is a fundamental unity of the one covenant of grace as it progressively unfolds throughout the Scriptures from Genesis 3:15 until its climax with the coming of Christ in "the fullness of time" (Gal. 4:4). Put in terms that relate to our topic of baptism, after the people of God placed the sign of the covenant upon their children for 2000 years, an explicit revoking of this practice is necessary if this practice is to end.[38] Continuity between the Old and New Testaments exists unless the New Testament states otherwise by revoking a practice. Those who deny infant baptism have labeled this an "argument from silence." But the silence is deafening! Arguments from silence are not weak arguments when it can be demonstrated that the reason for the silence is an assumed truth. The truth that the New Testament assumes from the Old is the biblical teaching that God has administered his covenant relationship with his people in essentially the same way. The form in which the covenant was administered changed from the Old Testament to the New, yet the substance of the covenant promise remains. This is why we say that there is and has only been one people of God throughout the ages, both in the Old and New Testaments. Listen to how this is so biblically stated by the Westminster Confession of Faith, chapter VII.5, 6:

> V. This covenant was differently administered in the time of the law and in the time of the gospel: under the law it was administered by promises, prophecies, sacrifices, circumcision,

---

38. This was also taught by the Reformer of Strasbourg, Martin Bucer (1491-1551) in his 1536 commentary on Romans, saying, "Since this had been the practice and observance of the Church as long as God's Church had been on earth, there was no reason why the Lord should issue special instructions about it in the day of a richer proclamation and fuller presentation of grace." *Common Places of Martin Bucer*, trans. and ed. D.F. Wright, *The Courtenay Library of Reformation Classics 4* (Appleford: Sutton Courtenay, 1972), 306.

the paschal lamb, and other types and ordinances delivered to the people of the Jews, all fore-signifying Christ to come, which were for that time sufficient and efficacious, through the operation of the Spirit, to instruct and build up the elect in faith in the promised Messiah, by whom they had full remission of sins and eternal salvation; and is called the Old Testament.

VI. Under the gospel, when Christ the substance was exhibited, the ordinances in which this covenant is dispensed are the preaching of the word and the administration of the sacraments of Baptism and the Lord's Supper; which, though fewer in number, and administered with more simplicity and less outward glory, yet in them it is held forth in more fullness, evidence, and spiritual efficacy, to all nations, both Jews and Gentiles; and is called the New Testament. There are not, therefore, two covenants of grace differing in substance, but one and the same under various dispensations.[39]

We see this unity taught clearly in the New Testament. In Romans the apostle Paul teaches that the nation of Israel should not be equated with the true seed of Abraham; that is, he rejected the belief that the physical descendants of Abraham were the spiritual people of the Lord. Instead, we are told that it is only the children of promise, those who believe in the Lord by faith alone who are "Israel," the seed of Abraham. This is why Paul calls Abraham "the father of all those who believe" (Rom. 4:11), not of all those who are physically or nationally descended from him. This is taught to us, for example, in Romans 9:6-8, which says,

But it is not as though the word of God has failed. For not all who are descended from Israel belong to Israel, and not all are children of Abraham because they are his offspring, but, "Through Isaac shall your offspring be named." This means that it is not the children of the flesh who are the children of God, but the children of the promise are counted as offspring.

"All Israel," that is, all ethnic Jews, were never all "of Israel," that is, of the true, spiritual Israel. This is how Paul answered

---

39. *Creeds of Christendom*, III:617-8.

the problem and disappointment of not seeing overwhelming conversions to Christ when he preached the gospel to the Jewish people.

The people of God are the people of faith. When Paul says in Romans 4:11 that Abraham is "the father of all who believe," whether uncircumcised Gentiles or circumcised Jews, he also says that the promise to Abraham to be "heir of the world" was not a result of his law keeping, but "through the righteousness of faith" (4:13). He then adds, "For if it is the adherents of the law who are to be the heirs, faith is null and the promise is void" (4:14).

Also think again of Romans 2:28-29. In discussing the high priority that the Jews placed on being circumcised, the apostle then responds by saying,

> For no one is a Jew who is merely one outwardly, nor is circumcision outward and physical. But a Jew is one inwardly, and circumcision is a matter of the heart, by the Spirit, not by the letter. His praise is not from man but from God.

This is why in Romans 11 Paul speaks of the "covenant tree." The root is holy and so are the branches (11:16) – but the branches are not made up merely of ethnic Israel, but Jews and Gentiles who have faith (11:20). His point is that the Gentiles, the wild olive branches (11:17), are grafted onto the *existing* olive tree and are nourished by it. The Church, then, is not a separate people, but the continuation of the one true people of God.

Paul continues this thought in Galatians 3:7 when he says, "Know then that it is those of faith who are the sons of Abraham." The entire context of 3:1-9, 16-19, 26-29, and 4:1-7 furnishes this view. We receive the Spirit "by hearing with faith" (3:5) just as Abraham "believed God, and it was counted to him as righteousness" (3:6 cf. Gen. 15:6). When God promised to bless all the nations of the world through Abraham in Genesis 12:3, he was pre-preaching the Gospel of grace to Abraham. These verses are so obvious in their meaning: God saved Abraham by faith by preaching the very same gospel to him that we hear; thus we are his spiritual children, members of God's one family. This is why Hebrews says, "For good news came to us just as to them" (Heb. 4:2). He also says that Christ, properly speaking, is the True Israel, the only True Israelite, the "Seed" promised to Abraham (3:16), and those who are "in Christ Jesus" are "sons of God" (3:26) - "And if you are Christ's, then you are Abraham's offspring, heirs according to the promise" (3:29).

So the true people of God in the Old Testament, who are descended from Abraham, are joined together by faith in Jesus Christ as God's people. And it is Jesus Christ, the "Seed," who is in effect the bridge between Old and New, Jew and Gentile. There is only one promise that the one, not two, people of God, cling to for salvation: Jesus Christ, the "Seed" promised to all generations, families, tribes, and nations from Genesis 3:15 until his glorious Second Coming.

This essential continuity and unity of God's people throughout both the Old and New Testaments was prophesied in Hosea 1:10-11, where we read,

> Yet the number of the children of Israel shall be like the sand of the sea, which cannot be measured or numbered. And in the place where it was said to them, "You are not my people," it shall be said to them, "Children of the living God." And the children of Judah and the children of Israel shall be gathered together, and they shall appoint for themselves one head. And they shall go up from the land, for great shall be the day of Jezreel.

Both Paul and Peter give us the inspired, authoritative interpretation of this prophecy. First in Romans 9:24-25 Paul quotes this passage saying that God has called not only the Jews but also the Gentiles. This passage is applied not to physical Judah and Israel, but as he has argued throughout Romans, those who are Jews inwardly (2:29). Peter quotes it in 1 Peter 2:9-10 where he attributes the titles of Israel in Deuteronomy 7:6 and Exodus 19:5-6 to the Church as well as

Hosea's prophecy, saying, "Once you were not a people, but now you are God's people; once you had not received mercy, but now you have received mercy."

Another prophecy of the unity between Old and New Testaments is the great "New Covenant" prophecy of Jeremiah 31:31-34. There the LORD, through Jeremiah, speaks to Judah and Israel, yet the writer to the Hebrews says this is fulfilled in the Church (Heb. 8:6-13), through Jesus Christ, the mediator of a better covenant (Heb. 8:6).

The prophet Amos also spoke in this way in Amos 9:11-15. His words were then interpreted by James at the first Church Council in Acts 15:13-17. The "booth of David" that Amos prophesied would be raised up again is declared by James to be fulfilled in the Church. How so? Christ himself is the true tabernacle of David, the true temple (John 2:18-22), who holds "the key of the house of David" (Isa. 22:22) in his hands (Rev. 3:7).

As a result of this unity of God's covenant promises throughout history and the unity of his people in both Old and New Testaments, there is much continuity between Old and New Testaments. Some aspects of the Old Testament religious system are abolished while many others are reinterpreted in a totally different way than we would ever expect. For instance, in the New Covenant we still worship at Mt. Zion, but it is now a heavenly mountain, a heavenly place (Heb. 12:22; Gal. 4:25-26; Rev. 3:12, 21:2, 10). The Church still worships at a temple, but because of Christ's once-for-all redemptive work, we as the Church of Jesus Christ are God's temple (1 Cor. 3:16; 2 Cor. 6:16; Eph. 2:18-22; Rev. 3:12). We still have a sacrificial altar upon which our Lord Jesus Christ was sacrificed, yet it is heavenly (Heb. 9:1-12, 21-24). The Holy of holies that the priest alone was allowed to enter into once a year under Old Covenant is now a heavenly place where all the redeemed may enter with boldness because Christ is our High Priest (Heb. 10:19-21).

Lastly, in Ephesians 2:11-22 Paul speaks about the joining together of the Jews ("the Circumcision") and the Gentiles ("the Uncircumcision"). Whereas the Gentiles were "alienated from the commonwealth of Israel and strangers to the covenants of promise" (2:12), they have now been made the people of God as Christ "has made us both one" (2:14). Christ united the Jews and Gentiles into the one people of God by abolishing the outward, ceremonial regulations of the Old Testament law. As a result, he has created "in himself one new man in place of the two" (2:15) so that "we both have access *in one Spirit to the Father*" (2:18). What a joy it is to know that we are "no longer strangers and aliens, but...fellow citizens with the saints and members of the household of God" (2:19), that we are "a holy temple in the Lord" (2:21), and that we are "a dwelling place for God by the Spirit" (2:22).

So the Scriptures teach that the one God has one promise of salvation and that all who believe in that promise are his people. This means that there are not two peoples of God, but one!

Promise & Fulfillment

As we come to understand this unity of the people of God throughout Old and New Testaments, we are led to the conclusion that this relationship is based on the fact that the covenant made with Abraham (Gen. 12, 15, 17) and the New Covenant in Christ is a relationship of *promise* and *fulfillment*. Basically, the New Testament teaches that the New Covenant is the Abrahamic covenant come to maturity.

We see this relationship in many Scripture passages. For example, in Mary's beautiful *Magnificat*, she praises God for using her to bring forth the Messiah. She says, "He has helped his servant Israel, in remembrance of his mercy, as he spoke to our fathers, to Abraham and to his offspring forever" (Luke 1:54-55). Luke records this promise/fulfillment relationship in the words of Zacharias' *Benedictus*:

> Blessed be the Lord God of Israel, for he has visited and redeemed his people and has raised up a horn of salvation for us in the house of his servant David, as he spoke by the mouth of his holy prophets from of old...to show the mercy promised to

our fathers and to remember his holy covenant, the oath that he swore to our father Abraham (Luke 1:68-70, 72-73).

These two beautiful poems teach that Jesus Christ, the mediator of the New Covenant, is the fulfillment of the ancient covenant promise that God made to his servant Abraham. Luke continues this theme of promise/fulfillment in the book of Acts 2:14-40, where the Holy Spirit was poured out upon the disciples. Peter defended against those who said they were drunk (2:15) by exclaiming, "But this is what was uttered through the prophet Joel" (2:16). He goes on to quote Joel 2:28-32 to show that this is the promise of the Holy Spirit and its fulfillment before their very eyes. He goes on to speak in this way with the resurrection of Christ (2:24-32) and His ascension (2:33-36).

In Acts 13:32-33 these very words, "promise" and "fulfillment" are used by Paul when he speaks about the resurrection of Christ saying, "And we bring you the good news that what God *promised* to the fathers this he has *fulfilled* to us their children by raising Jesus..."

When Paul stood before Agrippa in Acts 26 he also spoke in this way in the following words,

> And now I stand here on trial because of my hope in the *promise* made by God to our fathers...I will appear to you, delivering you from your people and from the Gentiles - to whom I am sending you to open their eyes, so that they may turn from darkness to light and from the power of Satan to God, that they may receive forgiveness of sins and a place among those who are sanctified by faith in me (26:6, 16-18).

It is interesting to see Paul speak of the promise to the Jewish fathers but then say it is fulfilled in his ministry to the Gentiles. He alludes here to the words of the prophet Isaiah (35:5, 42:7, 16), which promised that the eyes of the blind Israelites would be opened; but now he says it is fulfilled in the conversion of the nations! The true fulfillment is in the true Israel, all who believe, not all who are physically born as Jews!

Finally, this principle that the New Covenant Church is the

fulfillment of the Abrahamic Covenant taught by Paul in Galatians, where he says that the gospel preached to Abraham, of the *promise* of the inclusion of the Gentiles into Abraham's line, is *fulfilled* in us. Then he says in Galatians 3:13-14 that Christ was crucified in order that the blessing of Abraham (the *promise*) might come to the Gentiles (the *fulfillment*).

"Covenant Children"

Before we respond, "If it is only those who believe that are the true seed of Abraham, we shouldn't baptize our children until they believe," we need to take into account that both the Old and New Testaments teach that children of those who profess their faith are also members of the community. There is both a continuity between Old and New Testaments between those who believe being the true seed of Abraham, yet also, between the entirety of the Old Testament people being the people of God and the New Testament people being the people of God.

Some Christians, though, do not believe in infant baptism because they do not believe that children of Christians are a part of the covenant family of God. Here we want to examine what the Scriptures say as to whether *the children of believers are in the covenant family with their parents.*

Recall what I said in the opening of this book. Almost all Christians sing "Jesus Loves the Little Children" or "Jesus Loves Me" at baby "dedication" services, for example, in which they promise to raise their children *as Christians!* Whether one believes in infant baptism or not, there is inherently within the Christian a sense that our children are different from the children of the world and that we are to treat them differently.

This practice was true in all God's dealings with his former people. And what was true then is true now. In the writings of the New Testament we never read about Jesus or the apostles revoking the teaching that children of professing adults belong to the covenant people of God. Children are never said to be treated differently in the New Testament from the way they were in the Old. Never are we told that whereas the Israelite children were treated as part of the covenant community, the children of Christians are to be treated as outside the covenant community of Christ.

This would not have been difficult to do. After all, the New Testament records that many changes have occurred with the coming of Christ. Circumcision is no longer required of Gentile converts (Gal. 5); instead, both Jews and Gentiles who come to faith in Jesus Christ must be _baptized_ (Acts 2). Animal sacrifices are done away with because of Jesus' final sacrifice (Heb. 10). The kosher dietary laws no longer apply to the members of the Church because Jesus cleanses people from every tribe, tongue, language and nation and has declared all food good (Mark 7; Acts 10-11; 1 Tim. 4). The temple in Jerusalem is no longer the central meeting place between God and his people but is replaced by a "living temple" made up of people (Eph. 2; 1 Peter 2).

What we see throughout the Scriptures is that God works through family lines as covenant families. One merely needs to read the book of Genesis to see that children are considered to be within the covenant family. We begin with the "mother promise,"[40] Genesis 3:15: "I will put enmity between you and the woman and between your offspring and her _offspring._" Later God made his covenant with Noah, and his family. We read in Genesis 9:9, "Behold, I establish my covenant with you _and your offspring after you_" (emphasis added). When God called Abraham to be the vessel of his grace upon this sin-torn world, he continued his covenant with Abraham and his family, telling Abraham, "I will establish my covenant between me and you _and your offspring after you throughout their generations for an everlasting covenant, to be God to you and your offspring_

---

40. Herman Bavinck, _Our Reasonable Faith_, trans. Henry Zylstra (Grand Rapids: Eerdmans, 1956), 271.

after you" (Gen. 17:7; emphasis added). Later, towards to end of the Old Testament era, the prophet Isaiah foresaw the New Covenant era, in which, "All your children shall be taught by the LORD, and great shall be the peace of your children" (Isa. 54:13). This idea of the covenant including both adults and their children is much more than just an Old Testament teaching, though. We read of the magnificent promise of the Lord's grace at the beginning of the New Covenant in Acts 2:39: "For the promise is for you *and for your children* and for all who are far off, everyone whom the Lord our God calls to himself" (emphasis added).

Children are considered to be within the covenant[41] in the New Testament. We see this clearly in the writings of the apostle Paul. In Ephesians 6:1-4 and Colossians 3:20, Paul gives instruction on the responsibility of children to their parents, and their parents' responsibility to raise them. Notice how children are to obey their parents: "in the Lord" (Eph. 6:1). And as Colossians 3:20 says, "This pleases the Lord." We probably have read these passages more times than we can remember and possibly have overlooked this little phrase. In this case the saying "big things come in small packages" is true. In Ephesians 6:1 Paul uses the little preposition "in," which he uses in a multitude of places throughout Ephesians. It is used with the following direct objects in the Epistle to the Ephesians: "Christ" (1:3, 10, 12, 20, 4:32), "the blood of Christ" (2:13), "Christ Jesus" (1:1, 2:6, 7, 10, 13, 3:6, 21), "Jesus" (4:21), "the Lord Jesus" (1:15), "the Lord Jesus Christ" (3:11), "the Lord" (2:21, 4:17, 5:8, 6:10, 21), "him" (1:4, 9, 10, 2:15, 3:13, 4:20), "the Beloved" (1:6), and "whom" (1:7, 11, 13 [twice], 2:21, 22,

---

41. To be "within the covenant" simply means that God has a relationship with believers and their children and that they too receive the blessings of this relationship such as preaching, the sacraments, and Church discipline. This is no different than our children who belong to our family and receive love, shelter, and guidance although they may one day rebel or forsake their family.

3:12). He uses this prepositional phrase to describe the covenant relationship between Christ and his people. What Paul is saying is that we are his and belong to his body, the Church. "In..." is a shorthand way of saying that we are in the covenant of grace. For example, Paul says that we are blessed in him (1:3), elect in him (1:4), accepted in him (1:6), redeemed in him (1:7), have an inheritance in him (1:11), sealed with the Holy Spirit in him (1:14), and have been raised with him (2:6). All these are elements of what it means to be in the covenant of grace. So when Ephesians 6:1 says, "Children, obey your parents in the Lord" he is saying no small thing. The command to obey is based on the fact that children are in the covenant with their parents. As the children in the Old Testament were in the covenant with their parents, so too, Paul is saying, they are now. This is why Paul quotes the fifth Commandment, "Honor your father and mother" and says it still applies to children in the New Covenant. The command that applied to the covenant people (adults and children) then, is still true of the covenant people now.

This comes out so clearly when Paul says children who obey their parents "please the Lord" (Col. 3:20). We might simply ask, "How can this be true if the children of Christians are unbelievers and outside of God's family?" Paul himself speaks of the unregenerate world as those "in the flesh" who do not and cannot please God (Rom. 8:8). The only way to please God is to be in a covenant relationship with him. Thus, the apostle Paul is teaching us in this passage that our children are within the same covenant as we. As one writer states, when we see Ephesians 6:1-4 and Colossians 3:20 in light of Ephesians 1:1 and Colossians 1:1-2, it is clear that the covenant people of God includes children, or else why would Paul go out of his way to address the children of the congregation if they were not a part of it?[42]

---

42. M.J. Bosma, *Exposition of Reformed Doctrine* (4th edition; Grand Rapids: Smitter Book Company, 1927), 266.

Paul addresses this issue again in 1 Corinthians 7:14 in the context of the marriage between a believer and unbeliever, saying,

> For the unbelieving husband is made holy because of his wife, and the unbelieving wife is made holy because of her husband. Otherwise your children would be unclean, but as it is, they are holy.

Paul's point is that the family unit is "sanctified" even if only the husband or the wife is a believer. And so his conclusion is that even the children are "holy" as a result. He is not speaking of "sanctification" or "holiness" as he normally does, in the sense of the ongoing life of becoming more and more conformed to the image of Jesus Christ (e.g., Rom. 8:29), but in a typically Old Testament sense, that these types of broken, divided families are still covenant families.[43]

With regards to children, this text re-orients us from an individualistic mindset to a covenantal mindset. Scripture makes it clear that God is a covenant making God, and covenants include children. Thus our individualistic ideas of "making Jesus our *personal* Lord and Savior" and having a "*personal* relationship with Jesus" must be augmented. While we and our children are personally to embrace God's promises, the fact remains that God chooses to work through families. Thus, 1 Corinthians 7:14 says that children of believers, or even just one believer, are "holy" to the Lord. Just as the children of Israel were called "the holy seed" (Ezra 9:2; Isa. 6:13), so too the children of believers are called "holy" in the New Covenant era.

Finally, we see that the children of believers are "covenant children" in the attitude of Lord Jesus himself, who considered these children to be within the covenant community. He said, "Let the little children come to me, and do not forbid them; for of such is the kingdom of heaven" (Matt. 19:14 cf. 18:1-6; Mark 10:14-16; Luke 18:15-17). According to our Lord, children belong to the kingdom of heaven. When Jesus said this, he was

---

43. Kline, *By Oath Consigned*, 91-2.

rebuking his disciples' adult arrogance in trying to shield him from "insignificant" (in their minds) children. Instead, Jesus said, if we receive a child in Christ's name, we receive the Lord (Mark 9:36-37). But what does "in my name" mean? In verse 41 the Evangelist explains that to receive something in the name of the Lord means that it "belongs to Christ." So Jesus is saying that these covenant children belonged to him and thus the adult disciples had to become like them, insignificant, useless in the eyes of the world, and not claiming any worth in themselves in order to enter the kingdom of God. On this story of Jesus and the little children, Francis Turretin, one of the greatest Reformed theologians of the 17th century, said,

> Now if it was right for infants to be brought to Christ, why not also to be received to baptism, the symbol of our communion with Christ? Why should the church not receive into her bosom those whom Christ received into his? How unjust we should be to drive away those whom he willingly received.[44]

So why is all of this an important point to make? First, it teaches us that our God's covenant promises are unchangeable. He promised to include the children of believers in the covenant in the Old Testament, and because he does not change, neither does this promise.

Second, the Scriptures both of the Old and New Testaments make it absolutely clear that the children of believers are included in the covenant family of God. For us to deny this, is to deny the perspicuity and authority of the Scriptures upon our thoughts and lives.

Third, if these children are in the covenant, and all covenant members receive the sign of the covenant, then denying children the sign of baptism is to deny that they are in the covenant at all. To refuse them the sacrament is to treat the children of believers no differently than the children of

---

44. Turretin, *Institutes*, III:417.

unbelievers, despite the fact that Paul calls them "holy." It also denies their parents the enormous comfort of knowing that their children are included in the Church as recipients of God's promises.[45]

And so, the New Testament never says that the relationship of believers' children to the covenant community has changed. Therefore, just as the children of professing believers in the New Testament are said to be members of the covenant community as in the Old, so too these children are to receive the sign of being members of the community, just as the children inside the community did in the Old Testament.

Household Baptism

All that we have said about the covenant and the place of children within it can be clearly seen in the accounts of household baptisms in the New Testament. This is what has been called the *"oikos* formula."[46] *"Oikos"* is the Greek word that we translate "household." An *oikos* included the *pater familias,* or "father of the family," his wife, all children regardless of age, and all household servants and their families (as in the Old Testament). The point is not whether we can say there were children in this or that house, or servants and their families, but that households are mentioned along with the central authority figure of the house. And in order to have a household, there must necessarily be household subordinates

---

45. This also touches the issue of what we are to say to Christian parents who have lost a child. Our Reformed forefathers applied the teaching of covenant theology to this question in the Canons of Dort, I, 17, which says, "Since we are to judge of the will of God from His Word, which testifies that the *children of believers are holy, not by nature, but in virtue of the covenant of grace, in which they together with the parents are comprehended,* godly parents ought not to doubt the election and salvation of their children whom it pleases God to call out of this life in their infancy" (emphasis mine).

46. Joachim Jeremias, *Infant Baptism in the First Four Centuries,* trans. David Cairns (London: SCM Press, 1960), 20-4.

(wife, children, servants, and servants' family).[47] And so we will see below that there is a principle of covenant authority in the household established throughout the Old Testament, especially with Abraham.

The New Testament records eleven baptisms. Of these, five are of entire households *(oikos)*, three are of groups of people, the three thousand at Pentecost, the Samaritans (Acts 8:12) and the disciples of John the Baptist (Acts 19:1-5), and three are the specific accounts of individuals: our Lord (Matt. 3:13-17), who was fulfilling all righteousness in doing so as our Mediator, Saul (Acts 9:1-18), and the Ethiopian eunuch (Acts 8:27-38). Therefore we can say that h*ousehold baptism is the rule, not the exception!*

The five household baptisms are found in the following texts of the New Testament. First, Cornelius believed, was baptized, *and then his household was baptized.* In Acts 10:2 Cornelius and his family are described as God-fearing. Then in vv. 47-48 they are baptized. Then in Acts 11:14 we read the angel's message to Cornelius about Peter, "He will declare to you a message by which you will be saved, you *and all your* household."

Second, in Acts 16:14-15 we read that Lydia believed in the Lord, was baptized, and then her entire household was baptized as well.

Third, we read in Acts 16:30-34 of the famous "Philippian jailer" who believed *and then his entire household was baptized.* It is interesting to note the grammar of the text, which does not come out in the English translation. In Acts 16:34 Luke, the writer of Acts, uses a singular verb to speak of the jailer believing, but then mentions that the entire house is baptized. It cannot be said, "Well, he believed, then his household believed, then they were baptized," because the

---

47. Kline, *By Oath Consigned*, 97.

grammar says the jailer alone believed, and because of his belief, his entire household was baptized!

Fourth, we read in Acts 18:8 of Crispus' belief and his entire household's baptism.

Fifth, Paul says in 1 Corinthians 1:16 that he baptized Stephanus and his whole household.

By now you may be asking yourself, "But do not the 3000 baptisms on the day of Pentecost teach that only believers were baptized?" Surely this shows that people have to believe first, then be baptized. Irrespective of what we've just seen, the day of Pentecost records a great redemptive event, as the fulfillment of the Feast of Weeks (Pentecost) came to pass. This feast was one of the three obligatory feasts for all Israelites males (Ex. 23:14ff). Keep in mind, also, that the examples of conversions to Christ in the book of Acts are written within a *missionary* setting. The Gospel of our Lord was entering the lives of individuals, families, and communities for the very first time, so it would stand to reason that the emphasis we read of in the New Testament is of adults hearing the Word, believing the Word, and being baptized.[48]

Yet what is also telling for our purposes here is that although not explicitly saying that households were baptized on the day of Pentecost, in Acts 2:39 Peter proclaims that the promise of salvation was "for you *and for your children* and for all who are far off." This is a way of saying "you Jewish converts, your children (as with Abraham), and now the Gentiles." The phrase "all who are far off" comes from Isaiah 57:19 and is applied to the Gentiles in Acts 22:21, Ephesians 2:13 and 2:17.

---

48. "The New Testament record gives us the history of a missionary period, and in a missionary period, when the Church is being extended among those who before were outside, it is of course natural that predominant emphasis should be laid on the baptism of adults." M.J. Bosma, *Exposition of Reformed Doctrine*, 263; Turretin, *Institutes*, III:415.

We see this "theology of covenant families" all throughout the New Testament. Jesus could say to Zacchaeus, "Today salvation has come to this *house*" (Luke 19:9). In John 4:53 when Jesus healed the son of an official, the entire *household* believed. In 2 Timothy 1:16 Paul prays for mercy on Onesiphorus' entire *household*. In Hebrews 11:7-9 (cf. Gen. 7:1; 1 Peter 3:20-21) Noah and his family entered the ark because God found *Noah* righteous, and they all were saved because of his faith (1 Peter 3:20-21). In Matthew 10:12-14 the disciples were instructed to bless or curse *entire* households. This parallels the theology of the Old Testament. In Exodus 20:5ff the LORD punishes the sins of the fathers upon the children to the third and fourth generation of those who hate him, and shows mercy to thousands of generations of those who love him and keep his Commandments. On the Passover the children partook of the meal and were saved (Ex. 12). Rahab and her family were saved because of her faith (Josh. 2:13, 18, 6:23-25), and Joshua speaks of his entire house serving the LORD (Josh. 24:15).

And so we learn that household baptisms were commonplace in the New Testament and occur because of the conversion of the head of the household. Baptism does not, then, ever occur *apart from faith*, as many assume infant baptism teaches. We baptize the household of those who profess faith in Jesus Christ and who promise to raise their families in this faith. We do not baptize infants of non-Christian parents.

It is also a telling fact that while the New Testament records "household" baptisms, there is absolutely no evidence in the New Testament of an adult or older child, who had been raised in a Christian home but had not yet been baptized, who later is said to have been baptized *after* making a profession of faith in Jesus.

The Universality of Grace in the New Covenant

As we conclude this section of our study, let us reflect on a clear teaching of Scripture and how it affects our view of baptism. The book of Hebrews teaches that Jesus Christ is the mediator and guarantor of a better covenant with better promises (Heb. 7:22; 8:6, 13). Here the writer is contrasting the covenant with Moses, which he calls the Old Covenant, and the covenant with Jesus, the New Covenant. What we need to ask ourselves is whether we believe that the old, obsolete covenant with Israel had a more inclusive, universal grace.[49] What I mean is this: if the grace of God incorporated the children of the Israelites, their household servants, and their servants' children into the covenant people, why would we believe that the children of Christians are not to be included under the New and better Covenant, with a better mediator, and better promises?

Think for a moment about this question from the following angle. The Old Covenant was made with the Israelites; the New Covenant is made with Jews and Gentiles, the entire world. The Old was restrictive; the New is universal. Circumcision in the Old was a sign to only *male* infants; baptism in the New is a sign to *both* male and female infants (Gal. 3:28; Col. 3:11). The point is that infant baptism shows to us visibly the magnitude and endless bounds of God's grace.

So what we have seen is that circumcision and baptism are equated in the Scriptures as to what they meant. Baptism, as the sign of the New Covenant, replaces circumcision. As such, it is to be administered to all within the covenant family – whether adult or child. And this is evidenced in the ordinary accounts of New Testament household baptism. All of this shows us that while there is no text saying, "And Paul baptized the children," the baptism of the children of believers is built upon the good and necessary teaching of the Scriptures. Each piece of the biblical puzzle comes into clear view. Covenant baptism is undeniably biblical and not "Popery."

---

49. This question was discussed, and rejected, by Calvin, *Institutes*, 4:16:6. Cf. John Murray, *Christian Baptism* (Phillipsburg: P&R, 1980), 48-9.

Baptism or Dedication?

Now that we have investigated the key reasons for the baptism of covenant children, let us pause for a moment and answer a question that may be in your mind: "What about the practice of baby dedication?" This is important to discuss because for some this would seem to be more biblical than infant baptism as well as the fact that it is such a prevalent practice in our day.[50] Yet we need to mention by way of preface, that although dedication services are prevalent today, this is a very recent practice in Protestant churches, which should be cause enough to get us to pause and reflect upon it with some seriousness.

It bears repeating that the practice of baby dedication is evidence that many Christians believe their children are different from those of unbelieving parents. We baptize our children because we see them as members of the covenant. Why do Christians dedicate their children? If they do not believe their children are in the covenant with them, then they should not have them dedicated. As well, there is no basis to exercise any spiritual authority over their children since these children must be seen as little unbelievers outside the covenant and "in the world." On the other hand, if those who

---

50. One example of this practice among modern evangelical churches is Harvest Christian Fellowship, pastored by Greg Laurie, the preacher for the Harvest Crusades so popular in Southern California. On this church's website is a description of dedication, which cites the same texts Reformed churches cite for children being covenant children, and therefore proper recipients of baptism: http://www.harvest.org/knowgod/index.php/6/23.html

believe in infant dedication do believe the children of Christians are in the covenant with them, they should learn more about infant baptism, become consistent in their thinking and have them baptized!

Dedication in the Bible

The biblical "case" for baby dedication is by far much weaker than that of the baptism of covenant children. Although there are direct biblical examples of babies being dedicated in both the Old and New Testaments, nevertheless, they are never said to be a normative, ongoing pattern for Israelite or Christian children in the Old or New Testaments. Let us look at them for a moment.

Samuel

First, there is the dedication of Samuel by his mother Hannah (1 Sam. 1:11, 24-28). But notice that he was dedicated to do a priestly service in the LORD's house. She also dedicated him to be a "Nazirite" from birth, whose uncut hair signified his special consecration as a servant of God (Num. 6:1-21). Finally, Hannah's dedication of Samuel *did not replace his circumcision*, which was the sign of the covenant, as dedication replaces baptism today. This can hardly be seen as a pattern for baby dedication as none of the details of the text are followed in the services of dedication that occur today.

Samson & John the Baptist

Second, there are the examples of Samson and John the Baptist. Like Samuel, from their conception their parents dedicated them to the Lord. In fact, they were set apart by *God* to be Nazirites, and not by their parents, for the very specific redemptive purposes of being a judge and prophet, respectively (Judges 13:3-5; Luke 1:13-17).

So far Samuel, the great prophet of Israel, Samson, the final judge of Israel, and John, the last of Israel's prophets, are hardly biblical proof for the practice of baby dedication.

Jesus

Finally, there is the "dedication" of Jesus in the temple when he was 41 days old (Luke 2:22-24). He was circumcised at 8 days, and then 33 days later Mary could be "purified," according to Leviticus 12. Is this a biblical pattern for dedication? Again, it needs to be said that if we are going to use this as "proof," then we must follow the details of the text.

Instead, we see that Jesus' dedication involved the practice of ritual purification for Mary, which was an Old Covenant law that is no longer applicable today because Jesus has ended them! We also read in this story echoes to the Passover story, in which the Israelites' firstborn sons were to be redeemed by the sacrificing of an animal (Ex. 13:2, 15). Jesus' presentation in the temple is a prophetic fulfillment of the Passover lamb, as already from his infancy he is being set apart to the Lord as the final holy sacrifice (Ex. 13:12) and fulfilling all righteousness for us his people, obeying the Law of Moses.

What is so interesting about this purification ceremony is that the Belgic Confession of Faith cites it as evidence for infant baptism. After stating that our children are to receive baptism as the sign of the covenant, the Confession goes on to say,

> And indeed Christ shed His blood no less for the washing of the children of believers than for adult persons; and therefore they ought to receive the sign and sacrament of which Christ has done for them; as the Lord commanded in the law that they should be made partakers of the sacrament of Christ's suffering and death shortly after they were born, by offering for them a lamb, which was a sacrament of Jesus Christ.[51]

Christian "dedication" services, which may proof-text the above verses, do not follow the biblical pattern, which involved

---

51. *Creeds of Christendom*, III:427. As Venema correctly notes, this argument "is unique to the Belgic Confession among the Reformed confessions." "Sacraments and Baptism in the Reformed Confessions," 44, f.n. 26.

ceremonial purification of the child's mother after birth. Furthermore, dedication services do not involve offering sacrifices as the "example" teaches, for only Jesus' sacrifice on the cross can do that for us.

Baptism & Original Sin

Another reason infant dedication falls short of the purpose for which we baptize our children is the general biblical doctrine of "original sin." While this does not prove infants should be baptized, it acts as one of the many legs that hold up a table. Infant baptism is a testimony to our belief in our children being born in sin as children of Adam (Ps. 51:5).[52]

In the traditional service for covenant baptism in Reformed churches, the minister says to the congregation,

> And although our children do not understand these things [i.e., all that baptism means], we may not therefore exclude them from baptism, since they are without their knowledge partakers of the condemnation in Adam.[53]

Even as infants do not understand what it means to be a sinner, to place their faith in Jesus, and to live godly lives, so they do not need to understand what baptism is about. Put plainly, we do not need to know what it means to be a sinner in order to be a sinner. On the other hand, they are received in the grace of Christ's covenant people even before they can know what that means.

Infant baptism, then, is a testimony to the sovereignty of God's grace, in which he loved us before we loved him (1 John 4:10).[54] Dedication, on the other hand, is a testimony that the *parents* will raise this child. In baptism we see that God always initiates grace! He "came" to us first in eternity in his plan of election; he comes to us in the power of the Holy Spirit in

---

52. This argument was made by St. Augustine against Pelagius in the early 5th century.

53. "Baptism of Infants: Form Number 1." *Psalter Hymnal*, 124.

54. Warfield, "Christian Baptism," 328.

regenerating us from death to life; and he comes to us before we were even able to believe in him, by giving us the gift of faith so we may be justified. So too in baptism he comes to us first, even as we were helpless children, making a promise of grace to us.

Baptism & Justification

"Dedication" services, then, focus attention on the action of the parents. Infant baptism, on the other hand, focuses our attention and our hearts upon God's action, which we receive through faith alone. The baptism of children teaches that our children are sinful, and that they, along with the congregation, need to trust Christ alone for cleansing from their sins in order to be justified. Whereas dedication looks back and says, "We gave you to the Lord," baptism looks back and says, "The Lord gave himself to you in the promise of washing away your sins." Whereas dedication says, "We will raise you to trust the Lord," baptism says, "The Holy Spirit will raise you up from death to life to serve the Lord." The baptism of covenant children is the best dedication service possible, because God promises to dedicate himself to our children.

Baptism: Immersion, Pouring, or Sprinkling?

One general and practical concern about baptism that deserves a separate treatment is that of the *mode* of baptism. How is the water of baptism to be administered to converts and children of believers? Is it correct that immersion under water is the only proper mode by which to apply the water of baptism? Is it correct that if one is not baptized by immersion, then one was not truly baptized?

We have examined in some detail the meaning of baptism in Scripture, now we want to ask whether there is a biblical mode of baptism. As we approach this topic, the words of the great theologian of Princeton Seminary, B.B. Warfield, are instructive:

> [The New Testament]...simply commands that the disciples of Christ shall be introduced into their new relations by the rite of baptism; indicates incidentally that the element with which this baptism is to be performed is water; and, absorbing itself in the ethical and spiritual significance of the rite, leaves its externalities to one side.[55]

Three Biblical Modes

Baptism is legitimately administered by any of the three modes of immersion, sprinkling, or pouring. This was the

---

55. B.B. Warfield, "How Shall We Baptize?" *Selected Shorter Writings of Benjamin B. Warfield*, ed. John E. Meeter, 2 vols. (Phillipsburg: P&R, 1973), II:329-30.

judgment of the Reformed confessions,[56] the great Reformed theologians,[57] as well as our more recent theologians.[58] We can say this because baptism signifies not only our death, burial, and resurrection with Christ (Rom. 6), but also our cleansing from sin by the blood of Christ (Lev. 14:7; Num. 8:7; Ezek. 36:25; Heb. 9:13-14, 19-22, 10:22; 1 Peter 1:2), as well as our reception of the gift of the Holy Spirit who has been poured out upon us (Joel 2:28; Acts 1:5; 2:17-18, 33).[59]

What is important to grasp here is the classic distinction between the sign and the thing signified in the sacraments. The sign is the outward element, while the thing signified is the spiritual reality being portrayed. So what is the *sign* in baptism? We are basically asking the question whether the sign of baptism is the water or the way (mode) the water is applied. We

---

56. This is also the conclusion of the Westminster Confession of Faith, 28:3, which says, "Dipping of the person into the water is not necessary; but baptism is rightly administered by pouring or sprinkling water upon the person," in *The Creeds of Christendom*, III:662. As David Wright says, the Westminster Assembly was silent as to whether any particular mode was instituted by Christ. "Baptism at the Westminster Assembly," *The Westminster Confession in Current Thought*, ed. John H. Leith, *Calvin Studies VIII* (Davidson: The Colloquium on Calvin Studies, 1996), 86-7.

57. Hughes Oliphant Old, *The Shaping of the Reformed Baptismal Rite in the Sixteenth Century* (Grand Rapids: Eerdmans, 1992), 264-82; Geoffrey W. Bromiley, "Baptism in the Reformed Confessions and Catechisms," *Baptism, the New Testament and the Church*, eds. Stanley E. Porter and Anthony R. Cross, *Journal for the Study of the New Testament, Supplement Series 171* (Sheffield: Sheffield Academic Press, 1999), 408; *Sacramental Teaching and Practice in the Reformation Churches* (Grand Rapids: Eerdmans, 1957), 35.

58. Louis Berkhof, *Systematic Theology* (Grand Rapids: Eerdmans, reprinted 1994), 619; Venema, "Sacraments and Baptism in the Reformed Confessions," 70, 78; J. Van Bruggen, *The Church Says Amen: An Exposition of the Belgic Confession*, trans. Johanna VanderPlas (Neerlandia: Inheritance, 2003), 193; C. G. Bos, *Believe and Confess* (London, Ontario: Inter-League Publication Board, 2004), II:124-5.

59. It is interesting to note with regard to baptism by pouring (sometimes called, affusion), that Jesus' words, "You will be *baptized* with the Holy Spirit" (Acts 1:5) are described as the Spirit "coming upon" (Acts 1:8), "falling upon" (Acts 10:44, 11:15), and in Acts 2:17 (citing Joel 2:28 cf. Isa. 32:15; Ezek. 36:25-7) as "I will *pour out* my Spirit" (cf. Acts 2:33; Titus 3:5-6).

can answer this question by asking another: what does our Lord Jesus Christ's institution of the sacrament of baptism in Matthew 28:19 have to say about the mode of baptism? Jesus says nothing. The sign of baptism is the water, not the mode of the water's application.

Light From the Past

This has been the opinion of the historic Christian Church. In the earliest manual for church practice, the *Didache*, written sometime A.D. 80-120, the following is stated about the mode of baptism:

> 1. And concerning baptism, thus baptize ye: Having first said all these things, baptize into the name of the Father, and of the Son, and of the Holy Spirit, in living water [i.e., running water].
>
> 2. But if thou have not living [i.e., running] water, baptize into other water; and if thou canst not in cold, in warm.
>
> 3. But if thou have not either, pour out water thrice upon the head into the name of Father and Son and Holy Spirit (ch. 7).

Notice that the mode is indifferent. This document *preferred* baptism in a river of cold water, most likely to follow in our Lord's footsteps (but notice it doesn't say immerse in the river); yet, if this was unavailable, pouring water on the person somewhere other than a river was a legitimate baptism. In fact, the mode of pouring was the ordinary mode for baptism as far as we can tell from the early church.[60] Over a century later Cyprian of Carthage wrote to his son about those who were too sick and weak to be baptized in any other way than by sprinkling.[61]

The New Testament, therefore, along with the testimony of church history leads us to the conclusion that the mode of baptism is *adiaphora*, that is, a thing indifferent. Any of these

---

60. As Warfield states, "Affusion on the head of a recipient standing in shallow water, for instance, is the ordinary mode of baptism depicted in the early decorations of the Roman catacombs." "How Shall We Baptize?" 337.

61. Cyprian, *Epistle 69:12.*

three modes is legitimate, since each mode has biblical reasoning to support it as well as the fact that each mode points to some aspect of the spiritual reality of which baptism is a sign. This is belief is a part of our tradition, as evidenced by M. J. Bosma, one of the first Christian Reformed ministers to write in English. In his work *Exposition of Reformed Doctrine* he wrote,

> Is there only one mode in which baptism may be administered? No, it may be administered by immersion, by sprinkling or by pouring on water. The main idea to be represented is cleansing. How much water is used and how applied are matters of small moment.[62]

This indifference to the mode is seen in the words of several of the Reformers. This is what John Calvin wrote, when he said,

> Whether the person baptised is to be wholly immersed, and that whether once or thrice, or whether he is only to be sprinkled with water, is not of the least consequence: churches should be at liberty to adopt either according to the diversity of climates...[63]

Johannes Wollebius said "we use sprinkling, in a colder climate [i.e., Basel, Switzerland], with good reason, because of the weakness of children."[64] Finally, the great Reformed theologian of Geneva, Francis Turretin, said "baptism depends not on the quantity, but on the quality of water"[65] while Warfield said, "It is not the amount of water which we employ but the purpose for which we employ it."[66]

The mode of baptism is a matter of Christian liberty. No Christian should insist on any one mode as the only proper way

---

62. Bosma, *Exposition of Reformed Doctrine*, 259. See also the great Princeton theologian Charles Hodge, Systematic Theology, 3 vols. (reprinted; Grand Rapids: Eerdmans, 1995), III:526.

63. Calvin, *Institutes of the Christian Religion*, 4.15.19.

64. Johannes Wollebius, *Compendium Theologiae Christianae in Reformed Dogmatics*, ed. and trans. John W. Beardslee III (Grand Rapids: Baker, reprinted 1977), 130; Turretin, *Institutes*, III:381.

65. Turretin, *Ibid.*, III:381.

66. Warfield, *"Christian Baptism,"* 329.

for a legitimate baptism to occur. To do so is to make the traditions of men more authoritative than the commands of God and to tyrannize the consciences of those for whom Christ died. To make the mode of baptism necessary to salvation or membership in the Church of Jesus Christ "is opposed to the whole nature of the Gospel. It is to render Christianity more Judaic than Judaism."[67]

In saying this along with some of the greatest Reformed theologians we are not saying that because immersion is valid that we therefore reject or lessen the practice of infant baptism. A church may practice baptism by immersion and be completely distinguished from the theology and practice of Baptists. Examples of this would be the early practice of the church fathers, the practice of the Anglican Church in its early days, as well as the continuing practice of the Eastern Orthodox Church, which practices infant baptism by immersion.

A Look at Texts Used to Teach Baptism by Immersion Only

But what do we say about the texts of the New Testament that are said to teach baptism by immersion? For example, Matthew 3:6 and Mark 1:5 say that John the Baptist was baptizing "in the river Jordan." Yet note well that these verses do not say anything as to the mode John was using. If it is responded that John's baptizing where there was much water shows that this was because of immersion (John 3:23), it can be simply answered that because water supplies were precious, John would not go to a place without much water and so place hardship on that town. Furthermore, because people were traveling to hear John and be baptized by him, they would have needed water for themselves and their animals in order to survive.

A few more "conclusive" texts would seem to be Matthew

---

67. Hodge, *Systematic Theology*, III:526.

3:16, where Jesus "went up from the water" (cf. Mark 1:10) or Acts 8:38, where Philip and the Ethiopian eunuch "went down into the water..." and "...came up out of the water." Yet, these verses do not say that those baptized were immersed, but this is assumed. Keep in mind that the same argument those who are against infant baptism use to discredit the household baptisms in the New Testament ("They never say there were children with them"), can be used here. But, we do not even have to go that far. After all, we can just as easily read these texts to say that those baptized went down from the shore to stand "in the water" to have water poured over them; then we can understand them to have left the water and come back up upon the shore. Even more specifically, in Acts 8:38 the phrase "and they both went down" simply means that they stepped down from the chariot to the water below. As well, Acts 8:38 says both Philip and the eunuch "went down into the water." This cannot mean baptism by immersion, or else Philip baptized the eunuch and himself! This would mean that when we baptize, if we are to follow this example, both the person being baptized and the one doing the baptizing would have to go under the water.

What about 1 Corinthians 10? There we are told that the Israelites "passed through the Sea" (v. 1). Obviously they were not immersed as they passed through on dry ground (Ex. 14:22). But they were under sea level and hemmed in on both sides with water, right? Yes, but this would mean that people under sea level who do not get wet are baptized![68]

The two most common texts used to "prove" baptism by immersion are Romans 6:3-4 and Colossians 2:12, which speak of being buried with Christ in baptism. Again, these texts do not say those spoken of were baptized by immersion, but this is implied.

In Romans 6 Paul's point is that justified sinners (Rom. 5:1)

---

68. Murray, _Christian Baptism_, 22.

may not continue to sin so that grace may abound (Rom. 6:1). This is because we "died to sin;" that is, our guilt has been removed by Christ. Thus we cannot live in sin any longer because of Christ's work for us (Rom. 6:2). It is in this context that Paul introduces his discussion of baptism.

For Paul, baptism explains and gives meaning to his previous remarks, that justified sinners have died to sin. Christians are people who have been crucified with Christ (Rom. 6:6; Gal. 2:20), have died with him (2 Tim. 2:11), and were buried with him (Col. 2:12), and their baptism emphasizes that death. Thus to be baptized, is to be baptized into Christ Jesus, specifically into his death (Rom. 6:3), as he bore the curse of the Law for those who are lawbreakers.

But this is not the end of the story, for we are also baptized into his resurrection. We are also those who were made alive with Christ (Eph. 2:5; Col. 2:13), were raised with him to sit with him in the heavenlies (Eph. 2:6), are co-heirs with him (Rom. 8:17), sharers of his glory (Rom. 8:17), and those who will reign with him (2 Tim. 2:12).

According to Romans 6:5, if we have been united to Christ in his death and burial, we will be united to him in his resurrection. Thus, to enter the waters of baptism is to be united to Christ in his curse upon the cross. The irony is that, as God's people, we enter the waters of baptism in faith, believing that the covenant Lord himself will deliver us and our children from the curse by the very curse element itself – water, which consumed Pharaoh's armies while the people of God passed through safely (1 Cor. 10); which consumed the wicked world at the time of Noah while Noah and his family were saved (1 Peter 3:20-21). Believers in Christ and their children, enter the waters of judgment, in faith, believing that just as Christ died and was buried and rose again triumphantly, so too, we will escape God's curse by going through the ordeal with Christ.

So what these texts *do* say is that those baptized are baptized into Christ's death and resurrection. This is classic "sacramental language." What this means is that baptism is the visible sign, and the death and resurrection of Christ are the invisible things signified. This is why in Romans 6:5 Paul speaks of the visible sign of baptism uniting us to Christ's death and resurrection. Baptism unites us to the reality it signifies: Jesus' death and resurrection.

But doesn't the Greek word for "baptize" *(baptizo)* mean "to dip," or, "to immerse?" It is true that the ancient Greek root speaks of "dipping." There are ancient Greek writers that spoke of sunken ships and drowned sailors as being "baptized." Yet the use of the Greek word *baptizein* ("to baptize") was used by the Jews for "to purify" and "to cleanse." This is why Hebrews 9:10 speaks about the "various washings" (literally, "baptisms") of the Old Testament, as found, for example, in Exodus (19:14, 24:8), Leviticus (8:6, 30, 14:4-7, 16, 49-53, 16:19), and Numbers (8:5-7, 19:18, 19). As well, notice how this word is also used in Mark 7:3-4 and Luke 11:38 for the "washing" ("baptizing") of hands.

Two Quick Questions

To summarize, let us think about two questions. First, if immersion is necessary for a baptism to be valid, as it is said Romans 6 and Colossians 2 teach, then why isn't putting on a new pair of clothes after coming out of the water necessary? After all, Paul says in Galatians 3:27, "For as many of you as were baptized into Christ *have put on* Christ." Christ here is thought of as a garment enveloping the believer and symbolizing his new spiritual existence. This metaphor comes from the Old Testament where changing clothes represents an inward and spiritual change (cf. Isa. 61:10; Zech. 3:3f.).[69] Furthermore, in Romans 6 Paul does not only speak of being united with Christ's burial and resurrection, but also his

---

69. Ronald Fung, *The Epistle to the Galatians* (NICNT; Grand Rapids: Eerdmans), 172.

crucifixion" (Rom. 6:6). How is this signified in immersion? The point being that baptism signifies so much more than just merely our burial and resurrection with Christ and that to only look at two of the images in Romans and Colossians is arbitrary.[70] Shouldn't we be consistent and follow all that these texts supposedly say?

Second, if the mode of immersion is necessary for baptism, then why not for the other New Covenant sacrament, the Lord's Supper? After all, Jesus instituted his Supper at Passover (Matthew 26:17). Shouldn't we, then, partake of this meal once a year on the Passover? He institutes it at night (Matthew 26:20). This would mean the end of our "first Sunday morning of every month" practice of communion. Jesus gave his disciples holy communion while reclining at a table (Matthew 26:20). Should we get rid of pews? It was celebrated in an upper room (Mark 14:15). So do our church's need to be at least two stories tall? Jesus shared with his disciples a common cup (Matthew 26:27). Is this the end of individual plastic cups? As well, Jesus and his disciples most likely drank wine and ate the unleavened bread of the Passover.

These are important parallels to ponder so that we do not become overly divisive about the precise form of partaking of the sacraments. What is important is *what* they signify about Christ and his relationship to us and our relationship to his body, the Church.

---

70. Murray, *Christian Baptism*, 27-8 cf. *Collected Writings of John Murray*, 4 vols. (Edinburgh: Banner of Truth, 1977), II:372-3. This "arbitrariness" is shown, for example, in former Dallas Theological Seminary and Wheaton Graduate School professor Henry C. Thiessen's, *Lectures in Systematic Theology*, rev. Vernon D. Doerksen (Grand Rapids: Eerdmans, 1979), 325.

A Brief History
of Infant Baptism

As we near the conclusion of our study, we want to reaffirm that Scripture alone is the mine from which we dig the riches of God's self-revelation. As we study and attempt to interpret rightly Scriptures' teaching regarding infant baptism, we can glean much from the wise, studious men of God who preceded us in history. This doctrine will become clearer as we see how other godly men have understood it through the ages.

Many today claim that infant baptism began in the Roman Catholic Church and, therefore, it is to be disavowed. We do not practice this doctrine because we follow the Pope, but because it is in accordance with the Scriptures as historically understood in the Church. We see how others in history understood Scripture not as the standard of doctrine but as *testimonia veritas*, "testimonies of the truth."

In 1834, Samuel Miller, Professor of Ecclesiastical History and Church Government at Princeton Theological Seminary, said,

> I can assure you, my friends, with the utmost candour *[sic]* and confidence, after much careful inquiry on the subject, that, for more than fifteen hundred years after the birth of Christ, there was not a single society of professing Christians on earth, who opposed infant baptism on any thing like the grounds which distinguish our modern Baptist brethren.[71]

---

71. *Infant Baptism Scriptural and Reasonable* (Philadelphia: Presbyterian Board of Publication, 1834).

Here then is a brief survey of the ancient church fathers who lived from about A.D. 100-400. We do this to see the confirmatory witness of those who lived near the time of the apostles of the Lord. The following quotations will allow you to hear the fathers of the Church in their own words.

Irenaeus (120-202)

The first place we will look at is a brief paragraph by Irenaeus of Lyons, who lived from 120-202, and was a disciple of Polycarp, the bishop of Smyrna, who was a disciple of the apostle John. Irenaeus' testimony to the baptism of covenant children is found in these words:

> He came to save all through Himself, all I say, who through Him are reborn in God, infants, and children, and youth, and old men. Therefore He passed through every age, becoming an infant for infants, sanctifying infants; a child for children, sanctifying those who are of that age, and at the same time becoming for them an example of piety, of righteousness, and of submission; a young man for youths, becoming an example for youths and sanctifying them for the Lord.[72]

What these words show is the understanding in the early church that the children of Christians were viewed as Christian children, and not little unbelievers outside the covenant people.

Tertullian (160-230)

Next we look at Tertullian, who lived in the North African city of Carthage. He is often cited by Baptists as the first man to speak against infant baptism. While this was true later in his life, Tertullian acknowledged that infant baptism was the received practice of the churches, and he still encouraged it to be performed on babies who would not live past infancy. What he did teach later on in his ministry was that baptism should be delayed until later in life. Why did he say this? Because at that time the dominant belief in North Africa was that baptism washed away all sins up until that moment but not future sins.

---

72. *Against Heresies*, 2.22.4.

As a result, many waited until they were on their deathbed to be baptized; for example, the Emperor Constantine the Great. Tertullian never rejected infant baptism, but because of his theology, preferred that it be postponed until later in life.[73]

Hippolytus (170-236)

Another witness is Hippolytus of Rome, who displayed a clear, straightforward understanding of infant baptism when he stated, "And first baptize the little ones; and if they can speak for themselves, they shall do so; if not, their parents or other relatives shall speak for them."[74]

Origen (185-254)

Now we turn to Origen, who lived in Alexandria, Egypt and later in Palestine. He wrote in his *Commentary on Romans* of the connection between original sin and baptism, saying,

> For what is sin? Could a child who has only just been born commit a sin? And yet he has sin for which it is commanded to offer a sacrifice, as Job 14:4ff and Psalm 51:5-7 show. For this reason the Church received from the Apostles the tradition to administer baptism to the children also. For the men to whom the secrets of divine mysteries had been entrusted knew that in everyone there were genuine sinful defilements [sic], which had to be washed away with water and the Spirit.[75]

In another of his writings, his *Commentary on Leviticus*, he said, "According to the usage of the Church, baptism is given even to infants; when if there were nothing in infants which needed forgiveness and mercy, the grace of baptism would seem to be superfluous."[76]

Notice here what we said above about the link between original sin and baptism as Origen shows that the necessity of being forgiven of sin is a reason for baptism, and, which in fact,

---

73. *On Baptism*, 18.
74. *Apostolic Tradition*, 21.3-5.
75. Cited in Robert G. Rayburn, *What About Baptism?* (St. Louis: The Covenant College Press, 1957), 52.
76. *Homil. VII in Levit. Ch. 12.*

testifies of our need of a Savior. And so in his *Commentary on Luke* he reasoned,

> Infants are baptized for the forgiveness of sins. Of what sins? Or, when have they sinned? Or, can there be any reason for the laver in their case, unless it be according to the sense which we have mentioned above, viz: that no one is free from pollution, though he has lived but one day upon earth? And because by baptism native pollution is taken away, therefore infants are baptized.[77]

Whatever we make of the theology of these quotations as to the relationship between forgiveness of sins and baptism, we see the testimony of infant baptism from early on in the church as well as the logical necessity of baptism because of our original sinfulness.

Cyprian (200-258)

Cyprian, the bishop of Carthage, was martyred in 258. In his *Letter 58* he wrote to a pastor named Fidus. In this letter he drew upon the wisdom of sixty-six bishops at Carthage who had discussed Fidus' question of whether or not infant baptism should be delayed until the eighth day after birth instead of the usual second or third day. Their unanimous decision upheld the universally accepted practice of infant baptism, which they had always followed. The following points were given as to the reason for infant baptism:

> 1. Because God is no respecter of persons and his grace is universally given to all types, baptism ought to be administered to both adults and infants.

> 2. Because God is no respecter of persons and because his grace is universally given to all types, baptism ought to be given to adults and children and not limited to any particular age.

> 3. Because the grace of God is given to those who receive it in an equal measure, baptism ought to be given to both adults and children.

> 4. Since outward circumcision was abolished with the coming of Christ we are now given a "spiritual circumcision."

---

77. *Homil. in Luc. 14.*

5. Because God is no respecter of persons and because his grace is universally given to all types, baptism ought to be given to Jews and Gentiles alike: "spiritual circumcision ought not to be hindered by carnal circumcision."

6. If grace and baptism is given to those who commit heinous sins, "how much rather ought we to shrink from hindering an infant, who, being lately born, has not sinned, except in that, being born after the flesh according to Adam, he has contracted the contagion of the ancient death at its earliest birth."

Later in the city of Carthage, the leaders of the church met in 418 for the sixteenth Council of Carthage. That Council had to prevent a misunderstanding by some rural bishops, saying, "If any man says that newborn children need not be baptized...let him be anathema."

Polycarp (69-155)

Next we turn to three interesting lines of evidence from the ancient church to show that infant baptism was the standard practice. Polycarp, a disciple of the apostle John, was the bishop of Smyrna. In 155 he was martyred for his faith in Christ. The account of his martyrdom is moving:

> Now, as Polycarp was entering into the stadium...the tumult became great when they heard that Polycarp was taken. And when he came near, the proconsul asked him whether he was Polycarp. On his confessing that he was, [the proconsul] sought to persuade him to deny [Christ], saying, "Have respect to thy old age"..."Swear by the fortune of Caesar; repent, and say, 'Away with the Atheists.'" But Polycarp, gazing with a stern countenance on all the multitude of the wicked heathen then in the stadium, and waving his hand towards them, while with groans he looked up to heaven, said, "Away with the Atheists." Then, the proconsul urging him, and saying, "Swear, and I will set thee at liberty, reproach Christ;" Polycarp declared, "Eighty and six years have I served Him, and He never did me any injury: how then can I blaspheme my King and my Saviour?"[78]

---

78. *The Martyrdom of Polycarp*, ch. 9.

This is interesting because Polycarp said he served Christ for 86 years, the same amount of years he had lived, being born around A.D. 69. Joachim Jeremias, in *The Origins of Infant Baptism*, concluded the following from these facts,

> This shows at any rate that his parents were already Christians, or at least were converted quite soon after his birth. If his parents were pagans at his birth, he would have been baptized with the 'house' at their conversion. But even if his parents were Christians, the words 'service of Christ for eighty-six years' supports a baptism soon after his birth rather than one as a child of 'mature years'…for which there is no evidence at all.

Polycrates (130-196)

Another interesting line of evidence in this same vein comes from Polycrates of Ephesus. In 190, when writing to Rome concerning the dispute over the date of Easter, he stated that he was "sixty five years in the Lord." He was sixty-five when he wrote this and had been "in the Lord" for the same amount of time. What these two men's testimonies reveal to us is that their "spiritual birthday," if you will, began at their infant baptisms.

Justin Martyr (100-165)

One last line of similar evidence comes from Justin Martyr, a philosopher in Palestine who was converted to the Lord. He testified to the practice of infant baptism by stating, as above, "And many, both men and women, who have been Christ's disciples from childhood, remain pure at the age of sixty or seventy years."[79]

Augustine (354-430)

St. Augustine of Hippo, the great theologian and bishop of Hippo in North Africa, spoke simply of the baptism of children, saying, "For from the infant newly born to the old man bent with age, as there is none shut out from baptism, so there is none who in baptism does not die to sin."[80]

---

79. First Apology, ch. 15.
80. *Enchiridion*, ch. 43.

Yet he gave his greatest witness to infant baptism in his debates with Pelagius. As mentioned above, Pelagius denied original sin, that is, that children are born sinful. Yet, he practiced infant baptism. To this Augustine remarked on the inconsistency of this practice, for, after all, why are children baptized if they are not sinful?[81]

He also wrote about infant baptism being a universal practice of the Church since the time of apostles, saying,

> And this is the firm tradition of the universal Church, in respect of the baptism of infants, who certainly are as yet unable "with the heart to believe unto righteousness, and with the mouth to make confession unto salvation," as the thief could do; nay, who even, by crying and moaning when the mystery is performed upon them, raise their voices in opposition to the mysterious words, and yet no Christian will say that they are baptized to no purpose. And if any one seek for divine authority in this matter, though what is held by the whole Church, and that not as instituted by Councils, but as a matter of invariable custom, is rightly held to have been handed down by apostolical authority...[82]

Chrysostom (347-407)

Chrysostom of Antioch, in his 40th sermon on Genesis, commented on circumcision in this way,

> But our circumcision, I mean the grace of baptism, gives cure without pain, and procures to us a thousand benefits, and fills us with the grace of the Spirit; and it has no determinate time, as that had; but one that is in the very beginning of his age, or one that is in the middle of it, or one that is in his old age, may

---

81. *On the Grace of Christ, and on Original Sin*, 2.44; *On the Merits and Forgiveness of Sins, and on the Baptism of Infants*, 1.25, 3.2. This argument is also used by Jerome in his *Against the Pelagians*, 3.18.

82. *On Baptism, Against the Donatists*, ed. Philip Schaff, trans. J.R. King, rev. Chester D. Hartranft in *Nicene and Post-Nicene Fathers: Series 1* (reprinted; Peabody: Hendrickson, 2004), IV:461. In another of his writings, *On the Literal Interpretation of Genesis 10.39*, he says, "The custom of our mother church in baptizing infants must not be...accounted needless, nor believed to be other than a tradition of the apostles." See also *Letter 98*.

receive this circumcision made without hands; in which there is no trouble to be undergone but to throw off the load of sins, and to receive pardon for all past offenses."

The witness of the ancient Church was that baptism was to be administered to adult converts and their children. Whether we agree with infant baptism or not, we must agree that it was the practice of the post-apostolic Church, it was believed to be passed down from the apostles, and was never disavowed.

Inscriptions

Another interesting line of evidence of the practice of infant baptism in the early church is the many ancient inscriptions in the catacombs (underground cemeteries) and tombs of small children who had been baptized. As Everett Ferguson said,

> Early Christian inscriptions, which in the largest numbers come from the environs of Rome, furnish some instances of child and infant baptism for the third century...Nearly all the early Christian inscriptions are epitaphs. A considerable number of these are for the graves of children. The vast majority give no evidence whether the child was baptized or not...Actually the word "baptism" is seldom used. The idea is expressed by "received grace," "made a believer" or "neophyte" ("newly planted" used to mean "newly baptized").[83]

One such inscription from about A.D. 260 in North Africa indicates that a child who died nine hours after its birth was baptized and another calls a child *Dei Servus*, which means "slave of God."

As well, there are also Christian symbols on the tombstones of little children who had died, such as the *Chi Rho* symbol (the first two letters of "Christ") which stood for as an abbreviation for the name of Christ, and the Greek word *ichthus*, which was often symbolized by the "fish symbol." This was an alliteration to mean "Jesus Christ, God's Son, Savior." These words and

83. Everett Ferguson, *Early Christians Speak: Faith and Life in the First Three Centuries* (rev. ed.; Abilene: ACU Press, 1984) as cited at http://www.orlutheran.com/html/baptevid.html.

symbols are found on the tombs of children as young as a few days old.

One inscription from the 200's on a child's tomb says, "I, Zosimus, *a believer from believers*, lie here having lived 2 years, 1 month, 25 days" (emphasis added).

Sectarian Groups

One final note would be the interesting fact that during the period known as the "ancient Church" (A.D. 100-400) there were dozens of sectarian, unorthodox, and heretical groups such as the Ebionites, Novatians, Arians, Donatists, Montanists, and the Pelagians, who denied original sin. Yet none of these groups is known in all the ancient literature to have refuted the practice of infant baptism nor criticized those who did. In fact, with the Pelagians, they were even noted as practicing it, although, as we saw above, Augustine said this was inconsistent with his theology.

If infant baptism began *after* the death of the apostles, there surely would have been a controversy and debate within the churches. Yet, as we have seen, the only controversy in the early church over the baptism of infants was over the time between birth and baptism.

Before we reject a practice that has been performed in faithful Christian churches by the greatest theologians and pastors the world has ever known for 2000 years, we need to think long and hard about what that means for our individual and corporate faith.

A Word to Parents

We have examined biblical, theological, and historical foundations and evidence for the practice of baptizing the children of covenant families as well as a few practical and contemporary questions. The last thing we want to do is say a few words to prepare you for becoming covenant parents as well as presenting your covenant children to Christ in baptism. To do this we will utilize the "Address to the Parents" from the historic Reformed liturgy for baptism.[84] This order for the service of baptism was written by Petrus Dathenus (Peter Datheen) in 1566 and included in his Dutch Psalter for use by Dutch religious refugees in the German city of Frankenthal. It is a compilation of John Calvin's Genevan service, Johannes à Lasco's service for the Flemish refugees in London, the service from the German region of the Palatine, whose capital was Heidelberg, which can be traced back to Martin Luther and beyond.[85]

The basic pattern of this historic liturgical form is *instruction, invocation, vows, administration of baptism,* and finally, *prayer of thanksgiving.* In the instruction the minister first explains the meaning of baptism as teaching us about our guilt, the Triune God's grace, and our lifelong response of *gratitude*[86] and then he explains why we baptize the children

---

84. Baptism of Infants: Form Number 1." *Psalter Hymnal,* 124-5; see "Appendix 2" to this book.

85. *Psalter Hymnal Handbook,* Emily R. Brink and Bert Polman (Grand Rapids: CRC Publications, 1998), 831-2.

86. See Heidelberg Catechism, Q&A 2.

of believers. After the instruction the prayer of invocation follows.[87] In this prayer, the minister prays that the God who judged the world in the Flood, and Pharaoh's armies in the Red Sea, while saving his people through the very same waters (remember our discussion above about circumcision and baptism being both curse and consecration), would unite the child being baptized to Christ's death and raise him up in the newness of Christ's resurrection. After this comes the "Address to the Parents," which begins with a brief preface, saying,

> Beloved in Christ the Lord, you have heard that baptism is an ordinance of God to seal unto us and our seed His covenant; therefore it must be used for that end, and not out of custom or superstition. That it may, then, be manifest that you are thus minded, you are to answer sincerely to these questions:

Not Out of Custom or Superstition

Baptism is an "ordinance of God," that is, something our Creator and Redeemer has ordained and instituted, not man. As an ordinance, it was ordained in order to signify and seal God's covenant of grace unto us and our children.

For this reason, it is not a mere custom that gives you an opportunity to dress your children in white, to laugh and smile as they are held before the congregation, and to take pictures, nor is it simply a time to have a family reunion. Remember the words of Jeremiah 9:25-26 well. We too can run the risk of falling into the ungodly attitude and practice of viewing baptism simply as some outward rite, and thereby become "uncircumcised in heart."

Also, it is not to be done out of the superstitious belief that the water in any way washes away sins, brings the children to heaven, and guarantees salvation. After saying that the waters

---

87. This prayer, known as the "Great Flood Prayer" (German, *Sindtflutgebet*), was written by Martin Luther for his 1523 liturgy for baptism. See Old, *The Shaping of the Reformed Baptismal Rite in the Sixteenth Century*, 37-8, 227-33.

of baptism dramatically portray the cleansing of the souls from its sins, the Belgic Confession, in article 34, says,

> Not that this is effected by the external water, but by the sprinkling of the precious blood of the Son of God; who is our Red Sea, through which we must pass to escape the tyranny of Pharaoh, that is, the devil, and to enter into the spiritual land of Canaan.

Baptism, as we have said over and over again, points us to Jesus Christ. We are sinful, he is holy; we are disobedient, he was obedient; we are faithless, he is faithful. As you prepare for the baptism of your children, mark this well and ask the Lord to keep from you any idea of mere formalism, but that you would see baptism's true meaning and purpose.

The Vows

After this preface, the minister then asks three questions of the parents. These are sacred oaths not too be taken lightly. You are covenanting before God and his Church as you present your children for baptism.

Vow One

The first vow is meant to acknowledge the essential truths underlying infant baptism:

> First: Do you acknowledge that our children, though conceived and born in sin and therefore subject to all manner of misery, yea, to condemnation itself, are sanctified in Christ, and therefore as members of His Church ought to be baptized?

Our children are children of Adam and children of Christ. As children of Adam they are born in sin (Ps. 51:5) and deserve to be punished (Gal. 3:10). Our Belgic Confession, article 15 speaks of this "original sin," saying,

> We believe that through the disobedience of Adam original sin is extended to all mankind; which is a corruption of the whole nature and a hereditary disease, wherewith even infants in their mother's womb are infected, and which produces in man all sorts of sin, being in him as a root thereof, and therefore is so vile and abominable in the sight of God that it is sufficient to condemn all mankind. Nor is it altogether abolished or wholly

eradicated even by baptism; since sin always issues forth from this woeful source, as water from a fountain; notwithstanding it is not imputed to the children of God unto condemnation, but by His grace and mercy is forgiven them. Not that they should rest securely in sin, but that a sense of this corruption should make believers often to sigh, desiring to be delivered from this body of death. Wherefore we reject the error of the Pelagians, who assert that sin proceeds only from imitation.

Yet, despite our children being born into Adam's corruption, because they are born into covenant families, they are sanctified, that is, set apart from the world for Christ. As Paul says, this is true even if only one of the parents is a believer (1 Cor. 7:14). The conclusion is that as holy children, they are to receive the sign of their holiness, baptism. This is why our Canons of Dort, I, 17 says that "...the children of believers are holy, not by nature, but in virtue of the covenant of grace, in which they together with the parents are comprehended."

Vow Two

The second vow is meant to express your basic theological beliefs, as it asks,

Second: Do you acknowledge the doctrine which is contained in the Old and the New Testament, and in the articles of the Christian faith, and which is taught here in this Christian church, to be the true and complete doctrine of salvation?

As we said before, we do not baptize every child of every adult. In order to present a child for baptism, the parents must believe basic truths. First, you must acknowledge what the Bible teaches. In preparation for baptism, read Belgic Confession articles 2-7, which explain what we believe about the Word of God as God's self-revelation, which is inspired, canonical, authoritative, and sufficient. Second, you must confess the doctrine of the Word of God, which is summarized in "the articles of the Christian faith." This is how our Heidelberg Catechism, Q&A 22 describes the Apostles' Creed, the most basic of summaries of Christian doctrine. As well, you must affirm the doctrine of the Word as "taught here in this

Christian church." Make sure you are familiar with the Heidelberg Catechism, Belgic Confession, and Canons of Dort. In answering "yes" to this vow, you are acknowledging before God and his people that you are not presenting your children for baptism out of custom, having not come to church for years, nor being just a nominal member. Instead, you are confessing that you are a "living member" of the church (Heidelberg Catechism, Q&A 54) who confesses with the Body of Christ the truth of the Word of God in a dark world.

Vow Three

The third and final vow is meant to hear what you are going to do after your children are baptized, as it asks,

> Third: Do you promise and intend to instruct these children, as soon they are able to understand, in the aforesaid doctrine, and cause them to be instructed therein, to the utmost of your power?

Here is where the "rubber hits the road" for Christian parents. Baptism is not the end of the story, but the beginning, for both you and your children, as a lifetime of discipleship begins.

As Christian parents, it is your blessed duty to speak to your children about baptism just as Israelite parents spoke to theirs about circumcision. Hughes Oliphant Old summarizes the words of the Reformer Heinrich Bullinger, saying,

> It was after their circumcision that the children were taught what it meant. So also in the New Covenant we are responsible to teach our children the meaning of the sign, and to introduce them to the knowledge of the true Gospel.[88]

Speak to them about how baptism testifies of their sin, their

---

88. As summarized in Old, *The Shaping of the Reformed Baptismal Rite in the Sixteenth Century*, 132-3.

need of cleansing, and their inability to bring that about. Speak about how baptism portrays the washing that only Christ, by the power of his Holy Spirit, can give. Speak about how this washing is received by faith alone. Speak about how their baptism is a call to new life, daily putting off sin, daily crucifying the flesh, and daily following the Lord. Speak about how baptism is the promise that the Holy Spirit has been given to them to enable them to obey the Lord, love their neighbors, and give themselves as living sacrifices (Rom. 12:1-2). All this is beautifully portrayed in the "Collect for the Circumcision of Christ," from the 1552 *Book of Common Prayer*, which says,

> Almighty God, who madest thy blessed Son to be circumcised, and obedient to the Law for man; grant us the true Circumcision of the Spirit; that, our hearts, and all our members, being mortified from all worldly and carnal lusts, we may in all things obey thy blessed will; through the same thy Son Jesus Christ our Lord. Amen.

You can see you have some work ahead of you, but it is holy work, passing down the faith from generation to generation (Ps. 78) when you rise and when you lie down (Deut. 6) as you seek to raise your children in the "discipline and instruction of the Lord" (Eph. 6:4). This is why historic Protestant teaching emphasized the fact that baptism was not just a one-time ritual, not a custom, not a superstition, but a picture of the Christian life. Our Belgic Confession speaks of this life-long aspect of baptism, saying, "Neither does this baptism avail us only at the time when the water is poured upon us and received by us, but also through the whole course of our life" (art. 34). Baptism is the beginning of the Christian life of pilgrimage, from faith to faith, from glory to glory. This is why Martin Luther, in his *Large Catechism*, said,

> "Every Christian consequently has enough to learn and to practice all his life in regard to baptism...There is no greater jewel than Baptism for adorning our body and soul, for through it we become perfectly holy and are completely saved, something that otherwise no manner of life and no effort on earth can attain."

So be reverently joyful (Ps. 2:11) that God has blessed you with children of the covenant and that he uses *you* to bring about his eternal purpose in their lives.

Conclusion

So Jesus does love the little children, for "the Bible tells me so." This love has been shown as he has graciously included the helpless children of his professing people into his covenant family for thousands of generations, all throughout the Old and New Testaments. He shows us, and them, this truth in an outward, tangible way, by having his ministers place the waters of baptism upon them. In doing so, God testifies that although they are born sinners (Ps. 51:5), helpless spiritually, and in need of salvation, just as the rest of humanity, he accepts them as members of the household of God and surrounds them with all his promises and providences.

> Little ones to him belong
> They are weak, but he is strong.

Reformed Confessions on Baptism

appendix 1

French Confession of Faith, art. 35 (1559)

We confess only two sacraments common to the whole Church, of which the first, baptism, is given as a pledge of our adoption; for by it we are grafted into the body of Christ, so as to be washed and cleansed by his blood, and then renewed in purity of life by his Holy Spirit. We hold, also, that although we are baptized only once, yet the gain that it symbolizes to us reaches over our whole lives and to our death, so that we have a lasting witness that Jesus Christ will always be our justification and sanctification. Nevertheless, although it is a sacrament of faith and penitence, yet as God receives little children into the Church with their fathers, we say, upon the authority of Jesus Christ, that the children of believing parents should be baptized.

Belgic Confession, article 34, "Of Baptism" (1561)

We believe and confess that Jesus Christ, who is the end of the law, hath made an end, by the shedding of his blood, of all other sheddings of blood which men could or would make as a propitiation or satisfaction for sin; and that he, having abolished circumcision, which was done with blood, hath instituted the Sacrament of Baptism instead thereof; by which we are received into the Church of God, and separated from all other people and strange religions, that we may wholly belong to him whose ensign and banner we bear, and which serves as a testimony unto us that he will be our gracious God and Father.

Therefore he has commanded all those who are his to be baptized with pure water, *in the name of the Father and of the*

Son, and of the Holy Ghost: thereby signifying to us, that as water washeth away the filth of the body, when poured upon it, and is seen on the body of the baptized, when sprinkled upon him, so doth the blood of Christ, by the power of the Holy Ghost, internally sprinkle the soul, cleanse it from its sins, and regenerate us from children of wrath unto children of God. Not that this is effected by the external water, but by the sprinkling of the precious blood of the Son of God; who is our Red Sea, through which we must pass to escape the tyranny of Pharaoh, that is, the devil, and to enter into the spiritual land of Canaan.

Therefore, the Ministers, on their part, administer the Sacrament, and that which is visible, but our Lord giveth that which is signified by the Sacrament, namely, the gifts and invisible grace; washing, cleansing, and purging our souls of all filth and unrighteousness; renewing our hearts and filling them with all comfort; giving unto us a true assurance of his fatherly goodness; putting on us the new man, and putting off the old man with all his deeds.

Therefore, we believe that every man who is earnestly studious of obtaining life eternal ought to be but once baptized with this only Baptism, without ever repeating the same: since we can not be born twice. Neither doth this Baptism only avail us at the time when the water is poured upon us and received by us, but also through the whole course of our life.

Therefore we detest the error of the Anabaptists, who are not content with the one only baptism they have once received, and moreover condemn the baptism of the infants of believers, who, we believe, ought to be baptized and sealed with the sign of the covenant, as the children in Israel formerly were circumcised upon the same promises which are made unto our children. And, indeed, Christ shed his blood no less for the washing of the faithful than for adult persons; and, therefore, they ought to receive the sign and sacrament of that which Christ hath done for them; as the Lord commanded in the law, that they should be made partakers of the sacrament of Christ's suffering and death shortly after they were born, by offering for them a lamb, which was a sacrament of Jesus Christ. Moreover, what Circumcision was to the Jews, that Baptism is to our children. And for this reason Paul calls Baptism the *Circumcision of Christ.*

Heidelberg Catechism, Q&A 69-74 (1563)

69. How is it signified and sealed unto thee in holy Baptism that thou hast part in the one sacrifice of Christ on the cross?

Thus: that Christ has appointed this outward washing with water, and has joined therewith this promise, that I am washed with his blood and Spirit from the pollution of my soul, that is, from all my sins, as certainly as I am washed outwardly with water whereby commonly the filthiness of the body is taken away.

70. What is it to be washed with the blood and Spirit of Christ?

It is to have the forgiveness of sins from God, through grace, for the sake of Christ's blood, which he shed for us in his sacrifice on the cross; and also to be renewed by the Holy Ghost, and sanctified to be members of Christ, that so we may more and more die unto sin, and lead holy and unblamable lives.

71. Where has Christ promised that we are as certainly washed with his blood and Spirit as with the water of Baptism?

In the institution of Baptism, which runs thus: *Go ye, therefore, and teach all nations, baptizing them in the name of the Father, and of the Son, and of the Holy Ghost. He that believeth and is baptized shall be saved; but he that believeth not, shall be damned.* This promise is also repeated where Scripture calls Baptism the washing of regeneration and the washing away of sins.

72. Is, then, the outward washing of water itself the washing away of sins?

No; for only the blood of Jesus Christ and the Holy Spirit cleanse us from all sin.

73. Why, then, doth the Holy Ghost call Baptism the

washing of regeneration and the washing away of sins?

God speaks thus not without great cause: namely, not only to teach us thereby that like as the filthiness of the body is taken away by water, so our sins also are taken away by the blood and Spirit of Christ; but much more, that by this divine pledge and token he may assure us that we are as really washed from our sins spiritually as our bodies are washed with water.

74. Are infants also to be baptized?

Yes; for since they, as well as their parents, belong to the covenant and people of God, and both redemption from sin and the Holy Ghost, who works faith, are through the blood of Christ promised to them no less than to their parents, they are also by Baptism, as a sign of the covenant, to be ingrafted into the Christian Church, and distinguished from the children of unbelievers, as was done in the Old Testament by Circumcision, in place of which in the New Testament Baptism is appointed.

Second Helvetic Confession, ch. 20, "Of Holy Baptism" (1566)

Baptism was instituted and consecrated by God; and the first that baptized was John, who dipped Christ in the water in Jordan. From him it came to the apostles, who also did baptize with water. The Lord, in plain words, commanded them to preach the Gospel and to "baptize in the name of the Father, the Son, and of the Holy Spirit" (Matt. xxviii.19). And Peter also, when divers demanded of him what they ought to do, said to them, in the Acts, "Let every one of you be baptized in the name of Jesus Christ for the remission of sins, and ye shall receive the gift of the Holy Spirit" (Acts ii.38). Hence baptism is called by some a sign of initiation for God's people, whereby the elect of God are consecrated unto God.

There is but one baptism in the Church of God; for it is sufficient to be once baptized or consecrated unto God. For baptism once received does continue all a man's life, and is a perpetual sealing of our adoption unto us. For to be baptized in the name of Christ is to be enrolled, entered, and received into the covenant and family, and so into the inheritance, of the sons of God; yea, and in this life to be called after the name of God; that is to say, to be called a son of God; to be purged also from the filthiness of sins, and to be endued with the manifold grace of God, in order to lead a new and innocent life. Baptism, therefore, does call to mind and keep in remembrance the great benefit of God performed to mankind. For we are all born in the pollution of sin and are the children of wrath. But God, who is rich in mercy, does freely purge us from our sins by the blood of his Son, and in him does adopts us to be his sons, and by a holy covenant does join us to himself, and does enrich us with divers gifts, that we might live a new life. All these things are sealed up unto us in baptism. For inwardly we are regenerated, purified, and renewed of God through the Holy Spirit; and outwardly we receive the sealing of most notable gifts by the water, by which also those great benefits are represented, and, as it were, set before our eyes to be looked upon. And therefore are we baptized, that is, washed or sprinkled with visible water. For the water makes clean that which is filthy, and refreshes and cools and the bodies that fail and faint. And the grace of God deals in like manner with the soul; and that invisibly and spiritually.

Moreover, by the sacrament of baptism God does separate us from all other religions and nations, and does consecrate us a peculiar people to himself. We, therefore, by being baptized, do confess our faith, and are bound to give unto God obedience, mortification of the flesh, and newness of life; yea, and we are soldiers enlisted for the holy warfare of Christ, that all our life long we should fight against the world, Satan, and our own flesh. Moreover, we are baptized into one body of the Church, that we might well agree with all the members of the Church in the same religion and mutual duties.

We believe that the most perfect form of baptism is that by which Christ was baptized, and which the apostles did use. Those things, therefore, which by man's device were added afterwards and used in the Church we do not consider necessary to the perfection of baptism. Of this kind is exorcism, the use of lights, oil, spittle, and such other things; as, namely, that baptism is twice every year consecrated with divers ceremonies. But we believe that the baptism of the Church, which is but one, was sanctified in God's first institution of it, and is consecrated by the Word, and is now of full force, by the first blessing of God upon it.

We teach that baptism should not be ministered in the Church by women or midwives. For Paul secludes women from ecclesiastical callings; but baptism belongs to ecclesiastical offices.

We condemn the Anabaptists, who deny that young infants, born of faithful parents, are to be baptized. For, according to the doctrine of the Gospel, "theirs is the kingdom of God" (Luke xviii.16), and they are written in the covenant of God (Acts iii.25). Why, then, should not the sign of the covenant of God be given to them? Why should they not be consecrated by holy baptism, who are God's peculiar people ad are in the Church of God? We condemn also the Anabaptists in the rest of those peculiar opinions which they hold against the Word of God. We therefore are not Anabaptists, neither do we agree with them in any point that is theirs.

Westminster Confession of Faith, ch. 28, "Of Baptism" (1647)

I. Baptism is a sacrament of the New Testament, ordained by Jesus Christ, not only for the solemn admission of the party baptized into the visible Church, but also to be unto him a sign and seal of the covenant of grace, of his ingrafting into Christ, of regeneration, of remission of sins, and of his giving up unto God, through Jesus Christ, to walk in newness of life: which sacrament is, by Christ's own appointment, to be continued in his Church until the end of the world.

II. The outward element to be used in this sacrament is water, wherewith the party is to be baptized in the name of the Father, and of the Son, and of the Holy Ghost, by a minister of the gospel lawfully called thereunto.

III. Dipping of the person into the water is not necessary; but baptism is rightly administered by pouring or sprinkling water upon the person.

IV. Not only those that do actually profess faith in and obedience unto Christ, but also the infants of one or both believing parents are to be baptized.

V. Although it be a great sin to contemn or neglect this ordinance, yet grace and salvation are not so inseparably annexed unto it, as that no person can be regenerated or saved without it, or that all that are baptized are undoubtedly regenerated.

VI. The efficacy of baptism is not tied to that moment of time wherein it is administered; yet, notwithstanding, by the right use of this ordinance the grace promised is not only offered, but really exhibited and conferred by the Holy Ghost, to such (whether of age or infants) as that grace belongeth unto, according to the counsel of God's own will, in his appointed time.

VII. The sacrament of baptism is but once to be administered to any person.

Westminster Larger Catechism, Q&A 165-167 (1647)

Q. 165. What is baptism?

A. Baptism is a sacrament of the New Testament, wherein Christ hath ordained the washing with water in the name of the Father, and of the Son, and of the Holy Ghost, to be a sign and seal of ingrafting into himself, of remission of sins by his blood, and regeneration by his Spirit; of adoption, and resurrection unto everlasting life; and whereby the parties baptized are solemnly admitted into the visible church, and enter into an open and professed engagement to be wholly and only the Lord's.

Q. 166. Unto whom is baptism to be administered?

A. Baptism is not to be administered to any that are out of the visible church, and so strangers from the covenant of promise, till they profess their faith in Christ, and obedience to him, but infants descending from parents, either both, or but one of them, professing faith in Christ, and obedience to him, are in that respect within the covenant, and to be baptized.

Q. 167. How is our baptism to be improved by us?

A. The needful but much neglected duty of improving our baptism, is to be performed by us all our life long, especially in the time of temptation, and when we are present at the administration of it to others; by serious and thankful consideration of the nature of it, and of the ends for which Christ instituted it, the privileges and benefits conferred and sealed thereby, and our solemn vow made therein; by being humbled for our sinful defilement, our falling short of, and walking contrary to, the grace of baptism, and our engagements; by growing up to assurance of pardon of sin, and of all other blessings sealed to us in that sacrament; by drawing strength from the death and resurrection of Christ, into whom we are baptized, for the mortifying of sin, and quickening of grace; and by endeavoring to live by faith, to have our conversation in holiness and righteousness, as those that have therein given up their names to Christ; and to walk in brotherly love, as being baptized by the same Spirit into one body.

Baptism of Infants
Form Number 1

Instruction

Beloved congregation in the Lord Jesus Christ:

The principal parts of the doctrine of holy baptism are these three:

First: That we with our children are conceived and born in sin, and therefore are children of wrath, so that we cannot enter into the kingdom of God, except we are born again. This, the dipping in or sprinkling with water teaches us, whereby the impurity of our souls is signified, that we may be admonished to loathe ourselves, humble ourselves before God, and seek for our purification and salvation apart from ourselves.

Second: Holy baptism witnesses and seals unto us the washing away of our sins through Jesus Christ. Therefore we are baptized into the Name of God, the Father and the Son and the Holy Spirit. For when we are baptized into the Name of the Father, God the Father witnesses and seals unto us that He makes an eternal covenant of grace with us and adopts us for His children and heirs, and therefore will provide us with every good thing and avert all evil or turn it to our profit. And when we are baptized into the Name of the Son, the Son seals unto us that He washes us in His blood from all our sins, incorporating us into the fellowship of His death and resurrection, so that we are freed from our sins and accounted righteous before God. Likewise, when we are baptized into the Name of the Holy Spirit, the Holy Spirit assures us by this holy sacrament that He will dwell in us, and sanctify us to be members of Christ, imparting to us that which we have in Christ, namely, the washing away of our sins and the daily renewing of our lives, till we shall finally be presented without spot among the assembly of the elect in life eternal.

Third: Whereas in all covenants there are contained two parts, therefore are we by God, through baptism, admonished of and obliged unto new obedience, namely, that we cleave to this one God, Father, Son, and Holy Spirit; that we trust in Him, and love Him with all our heart, with all our soul, with all our mind, and with all our strength; that we forsake the world, crucify our old nature, and walk in a godly life. And if we sometimes through weakness fall into sins, we must not therefore despair of God's mercy, nor continue in sin, since baptism is a seal and indubitable testimony that we have an eternal covenant with God.

And although our children do not understand these things, we may not therefore exclude them from baptism, since they are without their knowledge partakers of the condemnation in Adam, and so again received unto grace in Christ; as God speaks unto Abraham, the father of all believers, and therefore also to us and our children, saying, *I will establish my covenant between me and thee and thy seed after thee throughout their generations for an everlasting covenant, to be a God unto thee and to thy seed after thee* (Gen. 17:7). This also Peter testifies with these words: *For to you is the promise, and to your children, and to all that are afar off, even as many as the Lord our God shall call unto him* (Acts 2:39). Therefore God formerly commanded to circumcise them, which was a seal of the covenant and of the righteousness of faith; as also Christ embraced them, laid His hands upon them, and blessed them (Mark 10:16). Since, then, baptism has come in the place of circumcision (Col. 2:11-13), the children should be baptized as heirs of the kingdom of God and of His covenant; and as they grow up, the parents shall be bound to give them further instruction in these things.

Invocation

That we, therefore, may administer this holy ordinance of God to His glory, to our comfort, and to the edification of the church, let us call upon His holy Name:

O almighty, eternal God. Thou who hast according to Thy severe judgment punished the unbelieving and unrepentant world with the flood, and hast according to Thy great mercy saved and protected believing Noah and his family; Thou who hast drowned the obstinate Pharaoh and his host in the Red Sea and led Thy people Israel through the midst of the sea upon dry ground – by which baptism was signified – we beseech Thee that Thou wilt be pleased of Thine infinite mercy, graciously to look upon these Thy children and incorporate them by Thy Holy Spirit into Thy Son Jesus Christ, that they may be buried with Him through baptism into death and be raised with Him in newness of life; that they, daily following Him, may joyfully bear their cross, cleaving unto Him in true faith, firm hope, and ardent love; that they, being comforted in Thee, may leave this life, which is nothing but a constant death, and at the last day may appear without terror before the judgment seat of Christ Thy Son, through Him, our Lord Jesus Christ, who with Thee and the Holy Spirit, one only God, lives and reigns forever. AMEN.

Address to the Parents

Beloved in Christ the Lord, you have heard that baptism is an ordinance of God to seal unto us and our seed His covenant; therefore it must be used for that end, and not out of custom or superstition. That it may, then, be manifest that you are thus minded, you are to answer sincerely to these questions:

First: Do you acknowledge that our children, though conceived and born in sin and therefore subject to all manner of misery, yea, to condemnation itself, are sanctified in Christ, and therefore as members of His Church ought to be baptized?

Second: Do you acknowledge the doctrine which is contained in the Old and the New Testament, and in the articles of the Christian faith, and which is taught here in this Christian church, to be the true and complete doctrine of salvation?

Third: Do you promise and intend to instruct these children, as soon as they are able to understand, in the aforesaid doctrine, and cause them to be instructed therein, to the utmost of your power?

Answer. We do *(or in the case only one of the parents is a confessing member:* I do*).*

Administration of the Sacrament
Then the Minister of God's Word, in baptizing, shall say:

N__, I baptize you into the Name of the Father and of the Son and of the Holy Spirit.

Thanksgiving

Almighty God and merciful Father, we thank and praise Thee that Thou hast forgiven us and our children all our sins, through the blood of Thy beloved Son Jesus Christ, and received us through Thy Holy Spirit as members of Thine only begotten Son, and so adopted us to be Thy children, and sealed and confirmed the same unto us by holy baptism. We beseech Thee also, through Him, Thy beloved Son, that Thou wilt always govern these children by Thy Holy Spirit, that they may be nurtured in the Christian faith and in godliness, and grow and increase in the Lord Jesus Christ, in order that they may acknowledge Thy fatherly goodness and mercy, which Thou hast shown to them and to us all, and live in all righteousness under our only Teacher, King and High Priest, Jesus Christ; and manfully fight against and overcome sin, the devil, and his whole dominion, to the end that they may eternally praise and magnify Thee, and Thy Son Jesus Christ, together with the Holy Spirit, the one only true God. AMEN.

Daniel R. Hyde (M.Div., Westminster Seminary California) is the Pastor of the Oceanside United Reformed Church in Oceanside, CA.